Best Practices

Published by
Applied Research and Design Publishing, an imprint of ORO Editions.
Gordon Goff: Publisher

www.appliedresearchanddesign.com
info@appliedresearchanddesign.com

Authors: Erin Besler and Ian Besler
Copy Editor: Courtney Coffman
Associate Editor: Christina Moushoul
Book Design: Erin Besler and Ian Besler
Project Manager: Jake Anderson

10 9 8 7 6 5 4 3 2 1 First Edition

ISBN: 978-1-951541-11-8

Color Separations and Printing: ORO Group Ltd.
Printed in China.

AR+D Publishing makes a continuous effort to minimize the overall carbon footprint of its publications. As part of this goal, AR+D, in association with Global ReLeaf, arranges to plant trees to replace those used in the manufacturing of the paper produced for its books. Global ReLeaf is an international campaign run by American Forests, one of the world's oldest nonprofit conservation organizations. Global ReLeaf is American Forests' education and action program that helps individuals, organizations, agencies, and corporations improve the local and global environment by planting and caring for trees.

This project was supported by a generous grant from The Graham Foundation for Advanced Studies in the Fine Arts.

Graham
Foundation

Best Practices

Erin Besler
and Ian Besler

Contents

Looking Around

Sylvia Lavin

Among the many forms of travel undertaken by modern architects, a particularly enduring type first emerged when the scientifically driven voyages of the architect/archaeologist established during the 18th century as a prerequisite to professional status converged with the grand tour needed for personal development according to the Romantic conventions of the 19th century.[1] This combination eventually produced a great literature of architectural books that are *Bildungsromans* as much as analyses of building practices. From Owen Jones's almost 10-year struggle to develop the technology adequate to represent the Alhambra to Richard Neutra's almost compulsive effort to detail *Wie Baut Amerika*, the formation of personal identity and the demonstration of professional mastery became entangled with the documentation of things learned on the road.[2] Despite some variation—Viollet-le-Duc famously rejected the architectural establishment's focus on classical antiquities and toured medieval France instead—the genre remained relatively stable in its triangulation of three constituent features: forms of observation and documentation modeled on scientific techniques and procedures, settings in unfamiliar terrains that present the geopsychic position of the author as unique, and a visual character shaped by an emphasis on technologies of representation and reproduction rather than on modes of drawing of immediate use to architectural practice.[3] The widespread consumption of these meticulously illustrated books exerted pressure on architectural practitioners by infiltrating an epistemic burden into the images that might otherwise have passed as mere tools of the trade.

The genre remained operative well into the 20th century, but as travel and photography became both easier and more ubiquitous, the triangulation of the component elements of architectural travel writing shifted. Scientific authority moved away from archeology and geology to ethnography and anthropology.[4] Unfamiliar settings were sometimes produced by psychic rather than physical travel, just as the documentary gaze turned from temporally as well as geographically distant monuments to local buildings. Giuseppe Pagano, for example, never left Italy in his effort to produce a comprehensive photodocumentary survey of vernacular architecture. But Pagano's work reflects the emergence of a new dimension to this form of architectural research: dispensing with the book as means of dissemination, Pagano published his findings through exhibitions and magazines, mediums that both facilitated and represented the growth in image travel.[5] Furthermore, this attention to innovation in and the popularization of diffusion intensified with increasingly easy access to photographic archives, decreases in print costs associated with images, and with the invention of inexpensive slide technology. Bernard Rudofksy, although eventually not only a life-long traveler but also a professional travel photographer, produced some of his most important research through armchair travel, scanning catalogs of photographic collections and travel books within reach of his desk. Rudofksy disseminated his findings in his exhibitions that themselves traveled.[6] These formats aimed in part toward larger and less professional audiences, recalibrated the relation between text and image that had typified the genre and its book format by reducing the number of words and increasing the number and size of printed images. These changes interrupted the conventions of literary narrative structure that had hitherto held sway in architectural travel writing and demanded new kinds of expertise. Mastering the art of visual juxtaposition and the pithy caption—"nature as architect" or "vernacular virtuosity"—and developing skills in image management—copyright, resolution, and sourcing—became forms of knowledge not only needed by architects within their practices but also proficiencies that led architects to new kinds of work as curators and editors.[7]

Ray and Charles Eames did not publish travel books, but they nevertheless published their travel extensively via exhibitions and lectures, often delivered by Charles using only a few notes. His *ex temp* oral style was reinforced by the way he used images—photographs and eventually slides were casually framed, as if also off the cuff, increasingly in color and so numerous that sometimes they were strung together into a filmic stream. This performance of an apparently automatic and animated unfolding of images, however, depended on a highly regulated system. The Eames Office was organized around managing an exhaustively large number of slides that seemed to document every moment of a trip. Slides were carefully choreographed by Charles for presentation and also strictly controlled by the office as if misplaced or scattered slides could disperse the Eameses themselves.[8] Although Charles did not photograph Los Angeles in particular, his work points to the formation of a new epistemology of the visual environment that sought to document the totality of a place or a subject through a virtually endless stream of images made possible by the cheapness of slides. Disposable images enabled even the most incidental of things to be captured and architectural authorship began to require skill in working not only with images as visible phenomena but also with the invisible systems that linked these images to the data that enabled them to function as signs and guarantors of authorship. As a result, if Rome satisfied the multiple psycho-technical epistemic demands made of the architect on the difficult road to professional development during the 18th century by offering universally recognizable monuments, the easy access to cars and roadways in Los Angeles invited anyone to document the total environment of the everyday and to make travel itself an everyday event. With a camera continually in hand, travelers of the 1960s were always ready to learn from whatever presented itself along a journey down the Sunset Strip.

Erin Besler and Ian Besler insert *Best Practices* into this concatenation of epistemologies and technologies undergirding the travel publications that have repeatedly been made by but have also repeatedly made modern architects. The Beslers considered describing the book as a photo-essay about the city of Los Angeles but realized that, for them, place is a flexible term: images of Rome pop in and out of their narrative, which is not really a narrative just as it is not really about the city of Los Angeles.[9] Instead, *Best Practices* is about the history of travel writing and especially the architectural photo-essays of the 1960s and 1970s that have been important to architects ever since, some of which are about LA but not produced by professional architects, such as those by Ed Ruscha, but also others made elsewhere linked to LA and its unmodernist character, notably Robert Venturi's *Complexity and Contradiction* and Venturi and Denise Scott Brown's *Learning from Las Vegas*.[10] The relation of *Best Practices* to these books is that of a software update to a precedent, a change to a source code: for example, the Beslers' return to Ruscha's *A Few Palm Trees* to find cell phone towers masquerading as palm trees and to Venturi and Scott Brown's neon signs, to find them in crumpled disrepair or replaced by vinyl stickers.[11] Like most updates, *Best Practices* is provisional: it lacks Ruscha's obsessive categorical clarity as well as Venturi and Scott Brown's confidence in the stabilities of architectural communication and, above all, anticipates it too will be found to have bugs that will need future updates. In keeping with this provisionality, the Beslers' attention is caught by what happens when categories collapse and communication fails. The book's graphic design causes the scholarly apparatus of footnotes to collide with emojis, and repeatedly shifts the fonts and orientations of the page; the book's language deploys formal terms to describe informal architectural accidents, like stucco spolia. And virtually all the Beslers' photographs document the architectural effects of collisions between bodies of knowledge — building codes versus construction know-how, the stability of architectural typologies versus the instability of weather, signage failures, climate adaptations, and interactions of "natural" and urban elements. "Document" is perhaps an overly structured word to describe the Beslers' images because they are evidence not of trips made with a destination in mind, but rather of the ubiquitous presence of the iPhone that makes every possible human movement into an opportunity to look around.[12]

In addition to being a retrospective look at how conceptual and pop art connect to architecture in its quotidian dimensions via their shared interest in the document, *Best Practices* is also a book about the coming of age in the iPhone era. The struggle to master and manage what was once a dispersed network of knowledge tools—from chromolithography to the jerry-rigged combination of camera and helicopter, slide tray, loupe, and index card—has been overcome by the omnipresence of the iPhone that compresses the expertise of producer, archivist, and publisher into a single, always at hand, thing.[13] In the media environment of the iPhone, Pinterest, and Tumblr's expanding list of an infinite array of categories make an artist's book about a few palm trees seem quaint, a trajectory towards the art market problematic, and the evidentiary value of any archive of images partial at best. In contrast, or perhaps in protest to the sleek design of the Apple and Google universe, the Beslers' images are prosaic and ungainly in the way they present prosaic and ungainly architectural and urban details. They are shaped not by the objective gaze of modern ethnography but rather by a gaze made suspicious by postmodern media theory's critique of the "artfulness" of cropping and centering and other techniques of formalization. Los Angeles operates as an incidental location, merely the place in which photographs of things that could be anywhere were taken. This casual attitude towards place uproots the psycho-geographic position of the Beslers and situates them not in an undiscovered utopia but instead within the anonymizing realm occupied by the "architects" of "door-esque" entries and "fleur-de-light switches." Instead, the book's title turns attention from the commercial boastfulness of the architecture of Best Products towards a form of conditional optimism, the best possible among not always satisfactory choices.[14] Most importantly, by moving away from the conclusiveness of a superlative product to the repetitive inconclusiveness of practices, this *bildungsroman* describes the pedagogical journey of an amateur.

While there are histories of amateurism in the arts, the professionalization of architectural knowledge during the 18th century has made the subject difficult for architectural historians. Originally, however, the architectural amateur was a person with respectable skill and talent but who was outside the institutions that directed young architects first to Rome and later to commissions; in other words, "amateur" was principally an economic rather than epistemological designation.[15] It became epistemological the more architecture was professionalized and the architect's education regulated. In this context, the amateur architect was uniquely free to travel along and hence learn from more undirected routes.[16] This peripateticism encouraged the development of the "looking around" technique, a phrase that came to mean "here and there with no fixed direction" precisely during the 18th century.[17] In *Best Practices*, the Beslers not only look at things made by amateurs—and travel through the world in undetermined and hence amateur directions—but they claim the amateur technique of "looking around" as a means of conducting architectural research in the digital media environment. The iPhone is the ideal instrument for the amateur architect because it enables "looking around" to seamlessly join looking at the world with looking at things on the internet, and also because it allows the activities of research, tourism, and daily life to be constantly recorded and immediately published to platforms like Instagram, where professionals and amateurs find each other once again as they did in the salons and studios of the 18th century.

Instagram is where the amateur comes of age. Many, if not all, architects use Instagram to advertise their professional services but it is the amateur architects who use Instagram and YouTube to share ideas, to consult with others, to suggest sources...to produce and disseminate knowledge. These platforms are driven by images, some manifestly mediated, and are therefore generally understood as important shapers of the post-literate and post-factual society, but new forms of textuality and pedagogy are also being invented for them. Memes, for example, are images endlessly redefined by the addition of new captions, texts that in effect become more definitive than the image.[18] Tags, comments, and DMs are dialogic discourses in which individual statements are evaluated not by their content but by the number of comments by others they trigger. Moreover, the ephemeral truths and provisional ideas trailing after Instagram images, a structure deployed by the graphic design of *Best Practices*, are important obstacles in their commodification and monetization—not only are the comments unending, but they operate under contradictory "ownership" rules and proprietary software that makes "collecting" them impossible, at least for now. Comments are thus "free," and unlike a label in a museum or a caption for a photograph, their value lies in constructing neither stable authors nor epistemes but in constituting an archive of potential and restless knowledge most accessible to the amateur who is "looking around." *Best Practices* documents the Beslers as they look around, write comments, and set the endless caption in motion to imagine it joining a vast information flow that both teaches and learns. How best to instrumentalize this as specifically architectural knowledge is not made clear, as has often been the case with travel literature, nor is this the Beslers' goal. However, it is also the case that in the digital media environment having the first word is a much more effective way of becoming an architect than having the last.

Notes

1. For the history of scientific travel and its impact on representation, see Barbara Maria Stafford, *Voyage into Substance: Art, Science, Nature, and the Illustrated Travel Account, 1760-1840* (Cambridge, MA: MIT Press, 1984). For various reconsiderations of the Grand Tour, see Gabrielle Brainard, Rustam Mehta, and Thomas Moran, eds., "Grand Tour," *Perspecta*, vol. 41 (2008). For more detailed histories of travel and architecture from the early modern to the invention of photography, see John Wilton-Ely, "Piranesi and the Role of Archaeological Illustration," in *Piranesi e la cultura antiquaria: gli antecedenti e il contesto: atti del convegno, 14-17 novembre 1979*, ed. Anna Lo Bianco, Palazzo dei Conservatori (Rome, Italy: Multigrafica, 1983); John Dixon Hunt, "The British Garden and the Grand Tour," *Studies in the History of Art*, vol. 25 (1989): 333–351; Karen Burns, "Topographies of Tourism: 'Documentary' Photography and The Stones of Venice," *Assemblage*, no. 32 (1997): 22-44; and Joan M. Schwartz and James R. Ryan, eds., *Picturing Place: Photography and the Geographical Imagination* (London: Tauris, 2003). For 20th century travel, see Jilly Traganou and Miodrag Mitrašinović, eds., *Travel, Space, Architecture* (Farnham, England: Ashgate, 2009).

2. On Jones, see Kathryn Ferry, "Printing the Alhambra: Owen Jones and Chromolithography," *Architectural History*, 46 (2003); and on Neutra, see Thomas S. Hines, *Richard Neutra and the Search for Modern Architecture: A Biography and History* (New York: Oxford University Press, 1982). See also Owen Jones, *Plans, Elevations, Sections and Details of the Alhambra, from drawings taken on the spot in 1834 by Jules Goury and in 1834 and 1837 by Owen Jones* (London: Owen Jones, 1842-45); and Richard Neutra, *Wie Baut Amerika* (Stuttgart: J. Hoffmann, 1927).

3. Viollet-le-Duc's decision to veer from the traditional Grand Tour is often linked to his decision not to train at the École des Beaux-Arts, which is to say that his travel and his formation as an architect are both fashioned out of this irregularity. Viollet's produced over 300 engravings and drawings, some of which were eventually published in Baron Taylor's *Voyages pittoresques et romantiques dans l'Ancienne France* (Leivarais, 1834). On these drawings, see Laurence de Finance, Jean-Michel Leniaud, eds., *Viollet-le-Duc: les visions d'un architecte* (Paris: Éd. Norma/Cité de l'architecture et du patrimoine, 2014); Viollet-le-Duc, Eugène-Emmanuel, Anatole de Baudot, and J Roussel, *Dessins Inédits De Viollet-le-duc* (Paris: Guérinet, 1902) as well as Jean Charay's introduction to the 1969 reedition.

4. See Emmanuel Amougou, ed., *Architecture et ethnographie au XIXe siècle: lectures des Conférences de la Société centrale des architectes français: Yvon Maurice (1857-1911), François-Adolphe Bocage (1860-1927), Jacques-René Hermant (1855-1930), Lucien Fournereau (1846-1906)* (Paris: Harmattan, 2008); and Elizabeth Edwards, "The Image as Anthropological Document: Photographic 'Types' and The Pursuit of Method," *Visual Anthropology* 3, no. 2-3 (1990).

5. Pagano ultimately became a photographer, in addition to being an architect. The entwining of these skills would shape the activities of young architects in Italy well into the century, a media trajectory that found its target, so to speak, in the work of the so-called radical architects educated at the University of Florence in the 1960s. On Pagano's photographic work, see Stefano Setti, "Double Vision Giuseppe Pagano and Franco Albini Photographers," *Figure*, Volume 3 (Dec. 2017): 73-84. On Pagano and other modern architects interested in the vernacular, see Michelangelo Sabatino, "Documenting Rural Architecture," *Journal of Architectural Education*, 63 (2020): 92-98; Francesco Passanti, "The Vernacular, Modernism, and Le Corbusier," *Journal of the Society of Architectural Historians*, vol. 56, no. 4 (1997): 438-451; Paola Tosolini, "Other Itineraries: Modern Architects on Countryside Roads," *The Journal of Architecture* 13.4 (2008): 427-51. See also Le Corbusier, *Journey to the East*, trans. Ivan Žaknić (Cambridge, MA: MIT, 1987).

6. On Rudofsky's travel, see The Getty Research Institute, *Lessons from Bernard Rudofksy: Life as a Voyage*, ed. Architekturzentrum Wien (Basel: Birkhäuser, 2007). See also Felicity Scott, "Bernard Rudofsky: Allegories of Nomadism and Dwelling," *Anxious Modernisms: Experimentation in Postwar Architectural Culture*, eds. Sarah Williams Goldhagan and Réjean Legault (Cambridge, MA: MIT Press, 2000).

   On traveling exhibitions, see Charles Musser and Carol Nelson, *High-Class Moving Pictures: Lyman H. Howe and the Forgotten Era of Traveling Exhibition, 1880-1920* (Princeton, NJ: Princeton University Press, 2016); Linda Risso, "Propaganda on Wheels: The NATO Travelling Exhibitions in the 1950s and 1960s," *Cold War History*, vol. 11, no. 1 (2011): 9-25; and Aaron Werbick and Andreas Müller, et al., eds., *Re-Reading the Manual of Travelling Exhibitions, UNESCO, 1953* (Leipzig: Spector Books, 2018).

   On armchair travel, see Carol Armstrong, *Scenes in a Library: Reading the Photograph in the Book, 1843-1875*, October Books (Cambridge, MA: MIT Press, 1998), 23-55; and Tom Gunning, "The Whole World Within Reach," *Virtual Voyages: Cinema and Travel* (Durham, NC: Duke University Press, 2006), 30-32.

7. These captions are from Bernard Rudofsky, *Architecture Without Architects: A Short Introduction to Non-Pedigreed Architecture* (New York, 1964), 20, 153—a publication that served as both an independent book and a catalog to the eponymous exhibition held at MoMA and then traveled extensively.

8. On the Eameses' travel to India in particular, see Saloni Mathur, "Charles and Ray Eames in India," *Art Journal* (Spring 2011). On visual technologies and the Eameses and more broadly during the post-war period, see Orit Halpern, "Perceptual Machines: Communication, Archiving, and Vision in Post-War American Design," *Journal of Visual Culture* 11:3 (2012): 328-351; and Jennifer F. Eisenhauer, "Next Slide Please: The Magical, Scientific, and Corporate Discourses of Visual Projection Technologies," *Studies in Art Education*, vol. 47, no. 3 (2006): 198–214.

9. This change was communicated to me in an email from Erin Besler on Feb. 11, 2021.

10. Denise Scott-Brown spent many years in Los Angeles teaching in the Urban Planning program at UCLA. She and Venturi were, in fact, married in her Ocean Park house on the West side of LA. Famously, Scott-Brown took students to Ruscha's LA studio before heading to Las Vegas. What became well known as Yale studio work—eventually published as *Learning From Las Vegas* by MIT Press in 1972—was an expansion of research Scott-Brown undertook previously while teaching at UCLA. On the Las Vegas work, see Martino Stierli, *Las Vegas in the Rearview Mirror: The City in Theory, Photography, and Film* (Los Angeles, CA: Getty Research Institute, 2013); and Aron Vinegar and Michael J Golec, *Relearning From Las Vegas* (Minneapolis, MN: University of Minnesota Press, 2009). On the relation between art and architects, including an essay on Ruscha by Susanna Newbury, see my book *Everything Loose Will Land: 1970s Art and Architecture in Los Angeles* (Nürnberg, Germany and New York, 2014).

11. Among the many artist books Ruscha made documenting things in multiples around Los Angeles, from apartment buildings to gas stations, was his *A Few Palm Trees* (Hollywood, CA: Heavy Industry Publications, 1971). Every spread has an address centered on the left of the page, and a single palm tree (or tree clump) also centered on the right, free-floating on the white page. Ruscha carefully edited the photographs by cropping out all traces of the visible city in the contact sheets. He also cut off the roots of the palm trees, which are of various species—most are not native to LA but rather brought to the city to beautify and improve its development during the early 20th century. Ruscha's "improvement" of the photograph in order to "beautify the tree," which requires such abstraction that the tree must actually die into order for it to become a sign, parallels the impact on living beings of urban development that turns land into real estate, hence the addresses on the left-hand side of the spread. Ironically, the development of art tourism, driven by the global celebrity of artists like Ruscha, has now turned Ruscha's addresses into destinations for taking selfies with what remains of the trees. The Beslers are precisely interested in such accretions.

12. There is a deep literature on the media archeology of the document, Lisa Gitelman's *Paper Knowledge: Toward a Media History of Documents* (Durham and London: Duke University Press, 2014) is an excellent source. For the relationship between the document and modes of writing that emphasize succinctness, like the memo, or in the case of this discussion, the caption, see John Guillory, "The Memo and Modernity," *Critical Inquiry*, Vol 31, No 1 (Autumn 2004): 108-132.

13. See also Peter Becker and William Clark, *Little Tools of Knowledge: Historical Essays on Academic and Bureaucratic Practices* (Ann Arbor, MI: University of Michigan Press, 2000).

14. Best Products, a catalog sales company that commissioned many of the most noted architects associated with postmodernism to design a national chain of showrooms, eventually lead to an exhibition held at MoMA, "Buildings for Best Products," in 1979. For an overview of the architecture of Best Products, see David Douglass-Jaimes, "When Art, Architecture and Commerce Collided: The BEST Products Showrooms by SITE," *ArchDaily*, Dec. 7, 2015, https://www.archdaily.com/778003/the-intersection-of-art-and-architecture-the-best-products-showrooms-by-site-sculpture-in-the-environment.

    On Venturi's travel to Rome and the American Academy, a journey also taken by the Beslers and hence no doubt the reason for the inclusion of Roman references in a book on LA—allusions that refer more to Venturi than to Rome—see Martino Stierli, "In the Academy's Garden: Robert Venturi, the Grand Tour and the Revision of Modern Architecture," *AA Files* 56 (2007): 42-55. On travel and the American Academy and architects more broadly, see Smilja Milovanovic-Bertram, "Learning from Rome," *Travel, Space, Architecture*, eds. Jilly Traganou and Miodrag Mitrasinovied (Farnham, England: Ashgate, 2009); and Denise Costanzo, "A Truly Liberal Orientation," *Journal of the Society of Architectural Historians* 74.2 (2015): 223-247.

15. Although there is growing literature on labor in architecture, including the work of do-it-yourselfers, anonymous workers, especially in corporate contexts, the work of women and people of color are not given access to the designation of architect, the category of the amateur remains unexamined in the history of architecture. For a discussion of the related idea of public education in the 18th century, see Reed Benhamou, "Cours Publics: Elective Education in the Eighteenth Century," *Studies on Voltaire and the Eighteenth Century*, no. 241, ed. Haydn Mason (Oxford, UK: Voltaire Foundation at the Taylor Institution, 1986), 365-76.

16. Viollet-le-Duc's tour of Southern France is the best-known example of this connection. See above.

17. In Middle English, "looking around" was principally a surveyor's term, a way of describing the action of moving along the edges of a property. The shift from a geographically-bound meaning to its opposite may be explained by shifts in the psychology of property. By the 18th century, a sense of ownership was often developed by the suppression of boundaries—through the use of ha-has, for example—and by the multiplication of vistas in as many directions as possible, in part produced by an increase in the number and size of windows.

18. Memes work in direct contradistinction to Rosalind Krauss's argument about the need to fix the indexical image to language by means of the caption. See her "Notes on the Index: Seventies Art in America Part 2," *October* 14 (Autumn, 1977): 58-67. On short writing and the internet, see Andrew Hui, *A Theory of the Aphorism: From Confucius to Twitter* (Princeton, NJ: Princeton University Press, 2019).

See and Say

Erin Besler and Ian Besler

For all of the liking, faving, friending, and following that pervades our experience of the world today—in the amorphous, constantly shifting, but always overlapping territory bridging "real life" with digital existence—it's striking how much architecture and design discourse can feel resolutely detached, inscrutable, unfriendly, and exclusionary. The most pressing questions facing contemporary architectural practice concern the perceived value of expertise and broader forms of knowledge that have been largely undervalued. Today these questions increasingly involve the role of media circulation and interactive platforms, which rapidly produce and proliferate new forms of specialization, socialization, and participation. However, prevailing biases of epistemology and academic discourse treat social media dismissively, as a superficial and undisciplined space to organize any serious research or analysis. Nevertheless, we regard the social media mindset as a cultivated form of knowledge production that engenders sophisticated strategies to construct and control meaning through image and text. Despite its proliferation and pervasive use across many forms of contemporary creative practice, cultural production, and visual communication, these impacts and implications have gone largely unaddressed in the field of architecture.

While the details of media culture and digital platforms are not the primary focus of this book, it is important to recognize their influence and impact on our inquiry, particularly how they interact with the built environment and architectural practice. Our conceptual point of departure for this project begins by acknowledging that the images we've assembled here were all captured for the express purpose of sharing on social media. As such, each image carries with it the residue of that space—each originally tailored, whether explicitly or implicitly, to generate "engagement."

The most remarkable aspect of digital interactions and social media, whichever app or other permutation it might be, is the self-asserting, ouroboros quality of the experience: The more you browse a social app, the more it trains you, and

More specifically: who has currency, representation, authority, and legitimacy to exert power, impart knowledge, and design buildings?

For more on this topic and YouTube instructional videos see our essay "Like So," Perspecta, no. 49, (2016): 214-218.

While architecture has its own memes, trending accounts, conversations, and viral topics, which work to reaffirm the shared conventions of image production and consumption, the effect has largely been to reinforce an echo chamber and reassert trends rather than create space for less recognized forms of production to enter, or for any meaningful discussion about it as a space for critical scholarly inquiry to occur.

… in turn, the more you train it. A simultaneous conditioning of vision and visual literacy into a myopia, or considered another way, an expertise, about what is and isn't suitable for successful circulation in that space. Browsing, clicking, scrolling, and sorting, however democratizing these actions may seem, are circumscribed by the biases, algorithms, and forms of AI built into each space. Each post, emoji, caption, like, comment, follow, and follow-back is a reification of its efficacy and influence. Although never explicit, every time we jab a thumb on our glowing, scrolling feed, beckoning a momentary pause in the stream and granting ourselves a second or two to consider the shared artifact—whether it be an architectural model, a cup of iced coffee, a weight room flex, a kooky cat, a façade detail, a makeup tutorial, a conspiracy theory, an advocacy campaign, an award-winning building, or a Renaissance painting—each and every post is always, inextricably a reinforcement of not only the "best practices" of visual expression, circulation, and production, but also of the more covert systems and structures defining these spaces. They often conclude with an endlessly reoccurring determination from each of us: to like or not to like.

In amassing this collection of charming, compelling, and otherwise idiosyncratic interventions and manifestations of the messy, curious, and quirky relationships between people and buildings, our focus is less on issues of content and engagement and more on the topic of "likeability." Each image is embedded with the motivation to garner likes, to be accessible, to be something around which people can orient themselves, and in turn, to motivate comments and follows. Yet, in their published incarnation on the following pages, we expect more from each of them. We imagine all of the images and texts presented here as probes, projected outward to measure the extents of "liking" and inclusion in architectural and design discourse. Like many other fields, architecture has its own particular, relatively narrow discipline and biased, exclusionary catalog of reference images. With each probe that finds purchase or promising ground, we see a new entry point into the field. This process rejects the isolationist approach so often characterized in architectural and design practices. Each entry calls out to validate and acknowledge a broader engagement with forms of knowledge that haven't been given meaningful attention or are only just emerging.

In certain cases, these probes may venture too far, farther than any reasonable expectation of solid footing. The territory beyond the "likeable" isn't simply inhabited by the

By now a controversial cliché, an emerging consensus settled on the claim that the current cultural moment is characterized by distraction, and the constant rivalries between feeds, push notifications, tabs, windows, devices, interfaces, and platforms are the source of a shared, day-to-day malaise, and an omnipresent sense of dissatisfaction. The quantification of attention, and its opposing condition of distraction, are now largely defined through "engagement." Influencers, creatives, brand ambassadors, promotional consultants, and other online entities pitched in an ever-evolving struggle, or so we're told, to maximize their audience's engagement with shared "content." The cold dispassion and cynicism of these terms—"content" and "engagement"—are captured in their capacity to package together eyeballs, pixels, ears, milliseconds, swipes, taps, …

… bots, and bodies into one catch-all unit of measure. Engagement marshals the forces of content to control attention while at the same time betraying a complete inability to recognize any meaningful distinction between people, actions, objects, and buildings. The series of images and texts we've assembled in the following pages are inextricably informed by this chaotic milieu.

… contemptible, as one might think, but rather by the unremarkable, the enigmatic, and the inane. Since we are designers, engaged with issues of form, expression, function, cultural values, and social situations, our first expectation of each image is that it can operate as a visually legible, intentional, and meaningful composition. Ideally, each entry is able to stimulate a line of associations and analogies that, when combined, can clarify into a novel synthesis. This relatively short-form, slightly meandering, "See 'n Say" approach to the structure and organization of the book opens a conceptual space to propose new ways of understanding the design of everyday spaces and ubiquitous objects. It provides an opportunity to address more nuanced and indefinite relationships between forms of power and how they manifest. It attempts to address the implications and possibilities of design in the era of late capital, amid the often inscrutable and obfuscated workings of class, labor, markets, inequity, sovereignty, and globalization.

This sense of ongoing calibration characterizes the project in terms of working through multiple varieties of image selections and arrangements, organizing and categorizing approaches, and generating textual associations through pairings with found quotations and our own writings, which also informs the book's title. The term "best practices" gained prominence in the 1990s through business publications and management seminars, embedding itself in the innocuous banter of professional jargon right up to the present day by virtue of its broad applicability across commercial fields. We are drawn to the term for the slightly beguiling friction it generates. Few common phrases use the adjective "best," particularly in the contexts of corporate communications. Instead, it brings to mind terms like "best friend" or "best buddy," an endearing classification of affections, suggesting there could be some application for sorting, ranking, or ordering one's most intimate fondnesses.

Best Practices provides a means for inserting a broader, more all-encompassing set of interests and references into contemporary architecture and design discourse. It's an invitation to thoroughly reconsider issues of expertise, professionalism, power, ubiquity, defaults, communication environments, construction practices, and how these things confront architecture. It's a way to level the playing field, or at the very least, a service door through which we can sneak our uninvited friends into the party, which is the field of architecture. It defines a territory within the margins

… between the sanctioned and unsanctioned, the regulated and unregulated, the tasteful and tacky, the novel and the nonsense. While not necessarily in opposition to those mechanisms, this book contends that interest, knowledge, and meaning are more often generated on the lines dividing such categories. This project advocates for a more thorough consideration of the unauthorized remodels, slap-dash handiwork, haphazard paint-jobs, half-hearted D.I.Y. projects, cracked facades, contradictions, compromises, and coincidences.

To convey the purpose and application for this collection of writing and imagery about the built environment, we stumbled through many terms: photo essay, design survey, architectural taxonomy, city guide, style primer, visual compendium, f.a.q., instruction manual, and others. In the end, "companion" seemed to fit best. It's a term steeped in the spirit of simultaneous affection and exhaustiveness, evoking a well of emotions we associate with deep fan cultures. While plenty of films and television shows have their attendant suite of "logs," production "guides," or "trivia" collections, only the most hopelessly nerdy artifacts of pop culture have "companions."☺ This companion is meant to move through the world, travel with you, offer new ways of seeing, and call attention to things that might not yet be entirely visible from the fields of architecture and design.

Many of the images depict facades or the finer points of houses, retail storefronts, warehouses, office parks, cars, street lamps, utility poles, traffic cones, statuary, topiary, ads, and various other examples of the ephemera that enliven and give dimension to architecture. Some of the images present lesser-explored details of well-known buildings, probing the limits of architectural authorship and influence, and the boundaries thought to separate design practices from the pragmatic concerns of construction trades and building regulations. Most of the images articulate and elevate the more humble, under-recognized forms of creativity and ingenuity, particularly with a view towards the forms of knowledge and access to resources thought to separate the expert from the non-expert.

More than two-hundred images were considered for inclusion in the book. Seventy-five made it to the final publication. All of them were captured with an iPhone camera between 2014 and 2019. The majority are of Los Angeles, Santa Monica, and the San Fernando Valley in California, but the collection also includes images of Mountain View, Chicago, Illinois, New

☺ Patrick McGoohan's The Prisoner or Rod Serling's The Twilight Zone, for instance.

... York City, and Syracuse, New York along with Naples, Rome, and Viterbo, Italy, as well as Sydney, Australia. While much of the writing and quotations address specific practitioners, buildings, design decisions, and artworks, or recount first-person experiences or historical events, the substantive relationships and meanings depicted in the images are found almost anywhere. As digital culture and social media allow these material and formal practices to proliferate well beyond any one specific site, the digital mediation current with day-to-day experience is increasingly reorganizing our shared perceptions and associations, particularly between architecture and place.

Best Practices: A Companion to Architecture... should be read as a joyful and enthusiastic approach to discover new meanings and practices of rewriting relationships within the ecosystem of architectural design, media, and culture. This encompasses both “IRL” and “extremely online” environments, which inform the attitudes, associations, and expression presented in this book. It uses irony and puns. It’s fun, and occasionally it makes fun. But we’ve worked to avoid the simplistic framing of sanctimony and judgment pervading design discourse. Conversations about “good design” and “bad design” are common because they demand little imagination or insight. They are problematic because they fail to consider the foundations and preconceptions on which those distinctions are predicated. And even the most cursory glance at the historical record reveals that “good taste” in architecture is rarely associated with good morals.

Erin Besler and Ian Besler

§ 1 - Austerities refer to any set of political economic policies that redirect government expenditure away from public interests. These constraints manifest in a built environment with frugal, formally oppressive finishes, stingy solutions, and inexpensive interventions related to economic practicalities, public resources, and capital flows. While the formal outcomes are often surprising and even charming in their indefatigable insistence on consistency, nevertheless the primary and problematic goal of austerity reinforces traditional class structures.

▲ **Religious ephemera**

▲ Given the degree to which religious structures have historically held the focus of architects—by way of treatises and conventions dictating plan, proportion, articulation, and other tedious issues—it seems somehow fitting that the contemporary church spire repeatedly bears the brunt of technological pragmatism with clustered accumulations of cellular and mobile data antennae, repeaters, wires, and mounting apparatuses.

It's as if the electrical engineers had finally pulled off their long-sought-after coup, leaping from the purely, insistently functional language of

… steel frames to the more ephemeral language of form by way of spirituality and the structures of organized religion. This phenomenon seems most common in relatively smaller towns (the photographed example here is in Syracuse, New York), though some notable examples can be found in Los Angeles.☆ Presumably, the tallest available space on an existing structure in a small town would tend to be water tanks or church spires, as opposed to skyscrapers or older radio towers in larger urban centers. One assumes, also, that small towns might be subject to diminishing rates of growth in both population and household income.

☆ See: For example, Iglesia de Dios de la Profecia on Hoover Street in Pico-Union or Holy Name of Jesus Church on Jefferson Boulevard in Jefferson Park.

These explanations could account for a religious congregation choosing to adorn their place of worship with cell signal equipment: the ephemera needed to access a plane of existence that increasingly demands more and more of our collective attentions, affections, and aspirations. Emojis and emails mingling with prayers and praise in various invisible and otherworldly ethers above congregants' heads, the church spire becoming a conduit for both simultaneously.

> “I muse along as quietly as a ghost. Instead of trying to sleep I try to fathom the mystery of this suburb at dawn. Why do these splendid houses look so defeated at this hour of the day? Other houses, say a 'dobe house in New Mexico or an old frame house in Feliciana, look much the same day or night. But these new houses look haunted. Even the churches out here look haunted. What spirit takes possession of them?”
>
> ▲ Walker Percy, The Moviegoer (New York: Vintage International, 1961), 86.

- - -  - - -

▲ **“House”**

▲ As with any act of modeling or depiction, choices have to be made regarding accuracy and fidelity in relation to the source material, evidenced here in a mock-up of a residential house exterior used for practice by Con Edison employees.

While the vinyl siding, soffit, and conduit remain true to scale, the roof, gable, and depth of the structure itself have shrunk, resulting in a bizarrely misproportioned building, which would otherwise feel insistently recognizable and stubbornly bland. It’s an austere version of the archetypal shape of a suburban house, where certain dimensions are accurate, but others appear

… strangely stretched and skewed,🠉 like a JPEG image that's circulated one too many times across screenshots, social media platforms, and devices—it's starting to show the sum of every transfiguration. The fussy attention to detail—evident in the choice of siding, trim, and the single-hung window—is endearing because it says that the depth of a structure is simply an optional variable, yet cladding details are specially privileged in the interest of depiction and simulation. This is an icon of a house, a simple graphic logo. But somebody misread the icon, mistaking it for an elevation, and then built the logo to scale.

🠊 This characteristic is also evident in houses designed for particularly narrow residential lots. For a few examples among many, see: "3106 St. Thomas," Office of Jonathan Tate, New Orleans, LA; "House and Garden," Ryue Nishizawa, Tokyo, Japan; "House K," Hiroyuki Shinozaki & Associates, Architects, Tokyo, Japan. See also: Erwin Wurm, "Narrow House," 2010, Venice Biennale, Venice, Italy; and 2015, Contemporary Art Centre, Vilnius, Lithuania.

> "Like the photograph in general, these houses bespeak a desire for projection beyond the limits of the familiar and known, perhaps even transcendence. Yet at the same time, they remind us just how thoroughly conflicted this impulse has always been, for we could just as easily read them as figures of containment and domestication. Echoing the borders of the print, these houses remind us as well to what extent photographic meaning is in fact a function of framing, excluding information, cutting the world off at the edges. In this way, they fold the limitless landscape in on itself, grinding it down."

▲ Jan Tumlir, "John Divola—The Social Degree Zero," in Isolated Houses, by John Divola (Tucson, AZ: Nazraeli Press, 2000).

- - -  - - -

▲ **Tiny house**

▲ Driving on a major roadway in Los Angeles—say on the I-10 heading east, toward Downtown—there are those very rare occasions in which you can find yourself almost completely alone on your own private stretch of highway.

These startling moments of isolation typically occur very late at night or perhaps early in the morning. The sight of eight vacated interstate lanes spread out in front of you—a space so regularly packed with the dispiriting monotony of SUVs, sedans, pickups, and semi-trailers—can feel downright surreal: an evacuated oasis in close proximity to a major urban center. The resulting feeling of irregular absence, like observing the low tide before a tsunami or finding oneself in the eye of a hurricane, while not quite so dramatically portentous, is still noteworthy for its capacity to turn an everyday

... context suddenly exceptional. Removing the cliché traffic congestion, for which the city is so famous, makes these moments stand out in one's memory.

Of course, unlike most other metropolises, the city throughout the LA River basin is broadly dispersed and mostly flat. Getting from place to place in a car involves negotiating the scarcity of traffic capacity across wide boulevards, occasional winding canyon roads, and the ubiquitous network of freeways. There are those noteworthy instances in the city's history in which the phenomenon of the vacated roadway has been intentionally enacted, when the flows of automobile traffic have been temporarily diverted, and the various boulevards and strips of concrete have been functionally turned over to an entirely distinct scale of movement: not so much mass transportation, but massive transportation.

In the late 19th century, it was surprisingly routine to see buildings making their way across Los Angeles. As redevelopment schemes and the encroaching pressures of commercial development extended outward, particularly from the neighborhoods around today's Civic Center east of Bunker Hill, many displaced residents brought their residences along with them. One imagines the vast majority of homes and other structures in these strategic strike zones of urban planning were simply demolished without any option of recourse; particularly in order to produce the unimpeded straight-shot lattice of the 10, the 110, the 405, the 710, and the 105 Interstates. As these roadways were forced in and imposed upon the region, historically significant architecture, local shops, and entire neighborhoods were destroyed.

For homeowners who could afford to relocate their properties during the boom era of skyrocketing real estate markets and explosive commercial business development, the migrating house became just another entity amid the bustling streets of the emerging metropolis. An industry emerged specializing in the relocation of houses. Lifted off foundations and propped up by a supporting wooden structure, a team of contractors, rollers, horses, and oxen would slowly inch the homes across the city, often hacking down tree branches and utility lines in their paths and temporarily reorganizing the still unstable patterns of the inchoate city. Picture a neat row of low-rise buildings with a solemn Victorian slowly rolling down the street in front of them. The scene evokes a sense of haunted wonder usually reserved for a Hayao Miyazaki film.

... More recently, these quirky historic parades were updated to reflect the bizarre abnormalities of late capitalism; the public spectacle of moving old mansions replaced with fine art and a mothballed spacecraft. In March 2012, a granite boulder almost exactly the size of a modest California bungalow arrived at the Los Angeles County Museum of Art campus on Miracle Mile after an eleven-day journey from a quarry next to Route 60 in Riverside. Only seven months later, the Space Shuttle Endeavor made a quicker, but equally idiosyncratic journey through the historically Black neighborhoods between Los Angeles International Airport and Exposition Park near the University of Southern California campus. Like the empty interstate occasionally encountered on a late-night commute, the image of an enormous spaceship lazily rolling past a row of storefronts seems to suggest that dedicating so much space to automobile traffic is undoubtedly the least interesting way to arrange the built environment.

▲ **Deterrent studs**

A surface covered with “anti-homeless spikes” is a kind of doppelgänger for the more benevolent surface covering of plastic truncated domes often found on the ground at pedestrian crossings and train platforms as helpful tactile indicators for the visually impaired.

See: § 4, “Accessible sewer” (pg. 110-112).

While walls, fences, and railings often perform a similar purpose as the studs, maliciously placed by property owners to deter unhoused people from entering and occupying a particular space, the bed of concrete spikes is far more punitive in how it formally embodies this task. In contrast to the graphic yellow color and rounded edges of the truncated dome, the hostile nature of the “anti-homeless spike” is a visual motif that explicitly conveys what is typically addressed in more circumspect yet insolent language (such as “urban renewal” of lower-income neighborhoods or “area cleaning” of “homeless encampments”)—an ideology that unjustly regards the built environment as a tool to be called upon to enforce cultural and economic barriers, as well as formal and functional barriers.

> “This artifact is a design object, the purpose of which is to punctuate architectural photographs. It has some utility as a bench, but is usually placed in isolation.”

William H. Whyte, Social Life of Small Urban Spaces. (Direct Cinema, Ltd., 1988), video [https://archive.org/details/SmallUrbanSpaces] 13:28-13:42.

--- ---

▲ **MY COMPANY NAME THERE**

Advertising slogans and commercial messaging can be so inuring that they become effectively invisible. As such, those rare encounters with nonsensical, filler sign copy ☞ can be delightfully memorable. The text acknowledges itself as completely superficial—a vaguely aspirational, even delusional endeavor. The lack of self-consciousness is always refreshing.

☞ See: For example, banners declaring "YOUR AD HERE," commonly deployed on bus benches throughout Los Angeles.

For instance, in a strip mall recently under construction near Chinatown in Los Angeles, large architectural renderings posted in the windows depicted each business as having the exact same storefront. Bold black-and-white lettering above each entryway simply read "Retail Store," as if that name alone could be sufficient (or desirable) for some small business, let alone every single business in a strip mall.

Displaying those renderings in the storefront windows seems one step short of actually creating the Potemkin storefront itself by hoisting the decorative signage for "Retail Store" up above the doorway and completely covering over the windows with more printed architectural renderings—images of well-stocked shelves, smiling store clerks, and customers shopping, chatting, and completing their illusory purchases. It's unsettling to imagine the proposition these renderings suggested: a strip mall where every single store shared the exact same sober and austere signage system, "Retail Store." It's like those strip malls in the suburbs where the developer has strong-armed every single tenant into using a uniformly sentimental, cloyingly nostalgic font and color scheme for their signage system, often involving half-hearted filigrees and fussy antiqued faux-bronze light fixtures that curve out over each store sign. By arbitrary force of will, on behalf of some fundamentalist property owner, the decades of (supposedly) invaluable brand identity work in which fast-food chains like McDonald's and Subway have invested can be erased, or at least, confused and curtailed. 🍽 In the interest of this one strip mall development that yearns to look like an "Olde Towne Square," the dry cleaners, the nail salon, the office supply store, and food outlets, are all forced into visual unison. The rich variety of formal language that typically defines our retail experiences is brazenly and dramatically decluttered; evidently, nostalgia doesn't have space for variety or nuance.

🍽 See: Famously the "Turquoise McDonald's," a corporate branding concession granted to satisfy the aesthetic desires of the Community Development Department in Sedona, Arizona; See also, § 5, "Paint Bucket Tool tolerance" (pg. 123-124)

--- ✹ ---

▲ **Clever disguise**

Like a few other bits of detritus in the built environment, communications equipment often betrays a staggering sense of indifference to the formal conventions of the material surfaces that so often host them. Sensors, antennas, signal amplifiers and the like seem to embrace a sort of aloof detachment in their relationships to the existing scenery, whether it be trees, church spires, ✞ or bricks.

Of course, bricks can always be deformed, ground down, and made to curve into a cylinder or a sphere, ❍ but the knowledge of such a gesture—if it were actually accomplished using the building material itself rather than through the application of a vinyl sticker—would be noteworthy and demand attention. When trying to blend into the surroundings, the irrational clumsiness of the gesture, "to hide" in this case, follows the logic of Adobe Photoshop's Paint Bucket tool, 🖌 wherein applying a texture map or pattern swatch that resembles brick, accomplishes the exact opposite effect. If this cylindrical plastic finial was instead made of actual bricks, as its surface treatment purports it to be, that would be exceptional! Here, it's simply an ornamental element that would otherwise go unnoticed. By inelegantly attempting to pass unseen, it somehow manages to call even more attention to itself.

- - - 🎭 - - -

✞ See: § 1, "Religious ephemera" (pg. 24-25).

❍ See: For instance, the work of sculptor Judith Hopf, or the cylindrical columns at Horrea Epagathiana and Epaphroditiana at Ostia Antica outside of Rome.

🖌 See: § 5, "Paint Bucket Tool tolerance" (pg. 123-124).

▲ **Extrusions by SketchUp**

▲ Los Angeles is replete with buildings that embody the formal qualities of a digital model created with SketchUp software, which is available for free online and primarily marketed to amateur, rather than professional, practitioners.

This visual association has nothing to do with the design or fabrication of these buildings (presumably the vast majority of buildings in the world have never existed as digital models, at least, not as part of the design process, but rather, were likely planned to the minimum degree allowed by local building codes and budgets). The "SketchUp look" is characterized by unorthodox relationships between proportions and surface treatments, as if imagined and iterated exclusively on the screen of a computer. An exemplar of the "SketchUp look" can be found in Rafael Viñoly's 432 Park Avenue tower, completed in 2015. The proportions are disconcertingly

... narrow and tall, and the enormous, unarticulated window openings only emphasize the sense of visual discord: as if a low-resolution rendering for a tower suddenly dropped into place at the edge of Central Park.

Note: 432 Park Avenue is currently among the first results that return in an internet search for the term "Pencil Building."
See also: Stefanos Chen, "The Downside to Life in a Supertall Tower: Leaks, Creaks, Breaks," The New York Times, Feb. 3, 2021.

> "As with other cities that have this new imagery, it looks stunning from the air but looks blocky when you get down low."

▲ Mickey Mellen, "New York City gets fresh 3D Imagery," Google Earth Blog, Apr. 15, 2013, web [https://www.gearthblog.com/blog/archives/2013/04/new-york-city-gets-fresh-3d-imagery.html].

> "I breathed in the night air that was or was not laced with anachronistic blossoms and felt the small thrill that I always felt to a lesser or greater degree when I looked at Manhattan's skyline and the innumerable illuminated windows and the liquid sapphire and ruby of traffic on the FDR Drive and the present absence of towers. It was a thrill that only built space produced in me, never the natural world, and only when there was an incommensurability of scale—the human dimension of the windows tiny from such distance combining but not dissolving into the larger architecture of the skyline that was the expression, the material signature, of a collective person who didn't yet exist, a still uninhabited second person plural to whom all the arts, even in their most intimate registers, were nevertheless addressed. Only an urban experience of the sublime was available to me because only then was the greatness beyond calculation the intuition of community. Bundled debt, trace amounts of antidepressants in the municipal water, the vast arterial network of traffic, changing weather patterns of increasing severity—whenever I looked at lower Manhattan from Whitman's side of the river I resolved to become one of the artists who momentarily made bad forms of collectivity figures of its possibility, a proprioceptive flicker in advance of the communal body."

▲ Ben Lerner, 10:04 (New York: Faber and Faber, Inc., 2014), 108-109.

--- \ ---

▲ **Helpful labeling**

The blunt immediacy of language in labels applied to buildings ("BLOCKED") seems especially reserved for points of ingress or egress.⇔

The management company for a building in Los Angeles's Jewelry District hangs signs across the glass entryway doors at night that read: "THIS DOOR IS CLOSED," which aspires to the blunt utility of "BLOCKED," but falls amusingly short of its aim due to the absurd obviousness of the message. Anyone can see that the doors are closed just by looking at them ("THIS DOOR IS LOCKED" is probably the less ambiguous message the management company intended to convey). As with the filler copy usually reserved for blank storefront signs,▤ it's interesting to imagine the other uses in which this kind of labeling could be applied, or a cityscape cluttered with equal amounts of signage and building. Such graphic applications start to turn buildings into signs, billboards, and diagrams, confusing the distinction between the plan and the built object.✚

\- - - - - -

⇔ See: For instance, "ENTER" or "EXIT," "OPEN" or "CLOSED," "CAUTION" or "CUIDADO."

▤ See: § 1, "MY COMPANY NAME THERE" (pg. 32-33).

For a specific typology map of signage in the city, see: "Strip Messages: Map of Las Vegas Strip showing every written word seen from the road," in Robert Venturi, Denise Scott Brown, and Steven Izenour, Learning from Las Vegas (Cambridge, MA: MIT Press, 1972), 20-21.

✚ See: § 1, "House" (pg. 26-27).

Bold lashes

From the vantage point of the public sidewalk, it's surprising how many charmingly slapdash and quirky examples of creative intervention can be found with just a cursory look. Treating a casual walk through the city as an opportunity for a contemporary anthropological survey of sorts reveals a typically overlooked and under-appreciated dialogue taking place between the public as consumers and the public as creators, designers, or that frustratingly broad catch-all: "makers."

Further, there seems to be a correlation between the status of objects and places as transitory and temporary, as not deserving of deeper formal consideration, and the unexpected materials and methods brought to bear

… on their configuration.🛠 For example, this often involves scrap lumber and some randomly applied hardware—like nails, angle brackets, bolts, and screws—to perform some structural adjustment, or the liberal application of packing tape, masking tape, duct tape, or rope. For the more invasively inclined, voluptuous globs of DuPont's Great Stuff™, PPG Industries' LiquidNails®, or 3M's Bondo® perform some inelegant, but nevertheless noteworthy, augmentation.

🛠 See: § 7, "Clipping mask" (pg. 172-174).

And what surface could be more transitory than the exterior of a car? Given the shameful inadequacy of transportation alternatives in most of the United States, the dependency on the automobile gives way to a remarkable sense of unsentimental practicality in how cars are made to look and function by their owners. Particularly in Los Angeles, and especially in those parts of Hollywood, Burbank, and Central LA that appear to be comprised of especially high volumes of auto parts stores and collision repair shops (one stretch of Pico Boulevard in Mid-Wilshire has at least a dozen auto body shops over a span of about three or four blocks), the parking spots that line most streets are a buffet of interesting creative examples. Of course, there's the classic "harlequin" body effect of mismatched hood, door, and fender colors as a result of multiple parts swapping—the car as a set of prefabricated, interchangeable components, rather than a single, indivisible whole. But then there are the more exceptional interventions: the headlight casing duct-taped into place, the rearview mirror reattached to the car door with a combination of wood screws and galvanized wire,⁂ or a crack in the fender sutured with steel staples and a globy smear of body filler.

⁂ See: § 7, "Suture" (pg. 161-163).

The reliably common nature of such details reflects a remarkable shift in the public imagination, one that still lingers as retroactively potent to Los Angeles' identity as a center of vanity "car culture" and the thoroughly antiquated idea of being a "gearhead." For most of us, any car manufactured in the past 20 years is an utterly inscrutable black box, wholly unsuitable for casual fine-tuning or modification. It should come as no surprise that the slapdash body adjustment, using off-the-shelf hardware and whatever all-purpose repair solutions we happen to have on hand, has become the new normal.

– – – 🚌 – – –

▲ **Door-esque**

There are often two overlapping dialogues that play out in the formal language of extremely functional spaces. The prosaic and unexceptional gestures on the one hand, and the painstaking integration of certain finish details on the other. This pattern is particularly evident in the treatment of drive-thrus, which organize circulation around so many banks and fast food outlets.

Here, for instance, it would have been unacceptably disruptive to our visual expectations of the building to have pragmatic concerns—such as the electrical access—made visible. And yet, we still see such details burdened (presumably by the demands of building codes) with clumsily showy door hinges and a label. It begs many questions: why not carry this logic forward with every single gesture? Why not call out each and every simultaneously hidden surface detail? Imagine: the floodlight above the door clad in tile and labeled; the bollards tiled and labeled; the curb tiled and labeled; the bushes tiled and labeled; the palm tree tiled and labeled. Apparently, some unspoken sense of propriety regulates where one logic ends and another begins.

(TL;DR: Why do buildings look the way they do?).

- - - ▯ - - -

See: § 3, "Obstructed view" (pg. 76-78).

See: § 1, "Helpful labeling" (pg. 38-39).

"Too long; didn't read," a shorthand popularized in online forums, and later on social media.

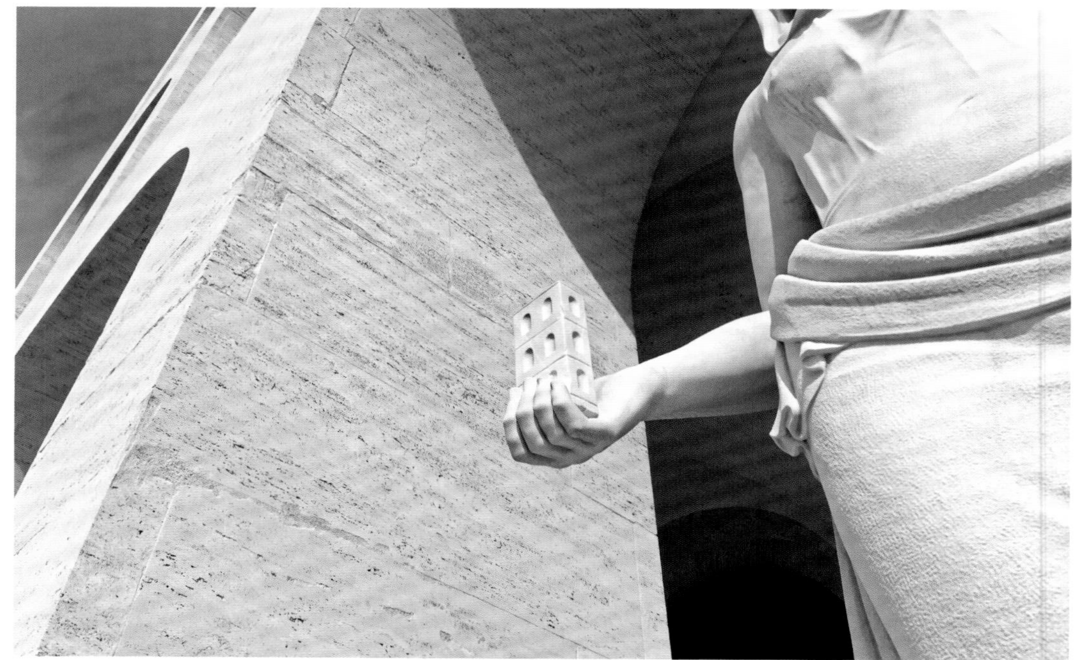

▲ **Handable architecture**

▲ There are entirely too few examples of scale models found within the actual buildings they depict. One can occasionally take comfort in the reliability of discovering a charming, Lucite encased, didactic scale model in a historic landmark building, a museum, or in the lobby of some starchitect's vanity condo tower project as a trophy or accessory. But otherwise, scale models as decorative elements are entirely underutilized, particularly for the talismanic qualities they seem to suggest.

While teaching mathematics in Gratz in 1595, Johannes Kepler realized that a circle drawn inside a triangle, then drawn inside a circle, described what he believed to be the relationship of the orbit of Jupiter to the orbit of Saturn.⊙ He would spend the following years attempting to model the solar

... system in such a way that the orbits of the six discovered planets could be described within a set of the five Platonic perfect solids, nested to fit the eccentricities of each planetary orbit.◎

Whereas nearly four hundred and twenty years later the dissemination of imagery and digital and physical models of intangible things (such as atomic structures and DNA helices) is relatively common, this procedure of physical abstraction and reduction based on relatively exact scientific accuracies would have been, presumably, a much rarer object of inquiry and mediation in the 16th century. But arguably, in our reading of them today, these objects perform similar functions as Kepler's planetary model did for him—they provide a rational, structured basis for the ongoing existence and accord of the natural world.

The scale model here takes on greater significance, not only in that Kepler saw it as a determinant of his aspired-for redemption in the mind of God, but that in eventually retreating from the nested Platonic model (though never explicitly rejecting it) and the false hope that it provided for a divine rationale to the universe, Kepler unknowingly asserted what would become the break between mysticism and science, astrology and astronomy. He provided a hypothesis and used the model as a tool for interrogating that hypothesis against his astronomical observations. When, after a great deal of frustration and deliberation, he finally concluded that his hypothesis and observations could not be reconciled, he withdrew his original hypothetical thesis, and in doing so, established a cornerstone of contemporary scientific inquiry. Here, the scale-model has been granted the capacity to communicate back. It becomes not just an object upon which logics and rationale are projected, but one which can get involved with its fabricator; even when, as in Kepler's case for so many years, the fabricator may not have the capacity to understand or internalize this affordance.⚒

> “Why look for two–dimensional forms to fit orbits in space? One has to look for three–dimensional forms—and, behold, dear reader, now you have my discovery in your hands!”
>
> ▲ Johannes Kepler, “Mysterium Cosmographicum,” Gesammelte Werke, Vol. I, eds. Walther von Dyck and Max Caspar, 1938.

⊙ See: Arthur Koestler, The Watershed: A Biography of Johannes Kepler (Garden City: Doubleday & Company, Inc., 1960), 43.

◎ See: Johannes Kepler, Mysterium Cosmographicum (Tübingen: 1596).

⚒ For an earlier and extended version of this text as well as an expanded discussion of scale models, see our essay “Some Scale Models We'd Like to Know,” San Rocco, no. 9 (2014): 86-93.

“ You can’t even imagine how big I can be...

...Cominciamo subito. Guarda la mia braccia nude. Posso abbraciare cento mille uomini stringere così. Quando muovo il fiancho, tremere i conventi...”

Let’s start now. Look at my naked arm. I can hold a hundred thousand men tightly in this way. When I move my hips, convents shake...

▲ Boccaccio '70 (1962, dir. Mario Monicelli, Federico Fellini, Luchino Visconti and Vittorio De Sica, Cinerez), 1:30:26-1:30:45.

“ Today we find the miniature located at a place of origin (the childhood of the self, or even the advertising scheme whereby a miniature of the company’s first plant or a miniature of a company’s earliest product is put on display in a window or lobby) and at a place of ending (the productions of the hobbyist: knickknacks of the domestic collected by elderly women, or the model trains built by the retired engineer); and both locations are viewed from a transcendent position, a position which is always within the standpoint of present lived reality and which thereby always nostalgically distances its object.”

▲ Susan Stewart, On Longing: Narratives of the Miniature, the Gigantic, the Souvenir, the Collection (Durham, NC: Duke University Press, 1993), 68–69.

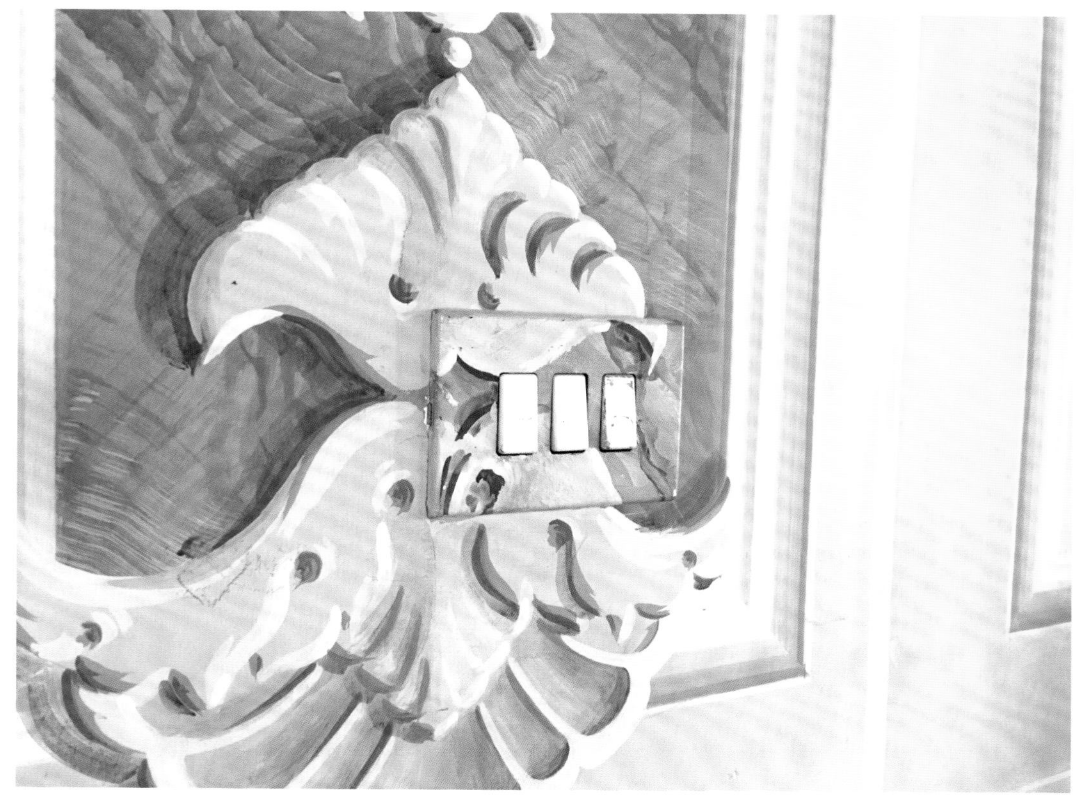

▲ **Fleur-de-light-switch**

▲ Gestures that tread the line between attention and compulsion ask the question: in our relationships with everyday objects, what are the qualities that merit care and consideration, over things that apparently deserve none?

Why are some affections and affinities appropriate, but other things—say, for instance, the uninterrupted continuation of a fleur-de-lis fresco of wall decoration across the trim plate of a light switch—are not? Perhaps

... this blurring of attentive boundaries is why Obsessive-Compulsive Disorder (OCD) occupies such a marquee status in the description of everyday anxiety and distress. It clarifies our relationships with objects and materials into a list of hierarchies; multitudes of different objects and surfaces that request or demand various degrees of our attention. Simply because a certain status is perceived as less desirable (the disruption of a wall decoration due to the position of a light switch), doesn't mean the way in which it communicates can't feel somehow refined and finished itself.

§ 2 - Well-calibrated yet unintentional, **coincidences** create charming juxtapositions between building elements—such as ornament, typology, and signage—with the unintended or uncontrollable effects of natural decay, weathering, accidental damage, or ill-fated choices. The whole is greater than the sum of its parts as new meanings and alternative readings can arise in places where they did not previously exist.

▲ **"Palm tree"**

▲ The word "coincidence" derives from the Latin word for "agree," then later, "to occupy the same space." We tend to think of coincidences in everyday life as phenomena marked by collision or contact, especially in terms of temporal and social relationships ("bumping" into a coworker on the street or "running" into a friend at the store, for example), yet the point of a coincidence is that the two objects in question cannot occupy the same space; in other words, they cannot be made to agree. Negotiating the

… coincidence becomes a visual manifestation of its inability to actually resolve into one, but rather to accumulate, to collect, to gather and occur, and to pile up, one on top of another.

Palm trees provide an emblem of coincidence in Los Angeles. Although only the desert fan palm (Washingtonia filifera) is native to the region, an enormous variety of palm species were sought after and cultivated in the city over the past century. Owing to their instant recognizability as icons of inviting and temperate climates, the palm eventually became an indispensable ingredient in the public imaginary of the city.

Following the era of Boosterism and postcard marketing in the late 19th century and early 20th century, developers and landscapers planted thousands of palms across the city, specifically in anticipation of the 1932 Olympic games. The palms were coincidentally well-timed to play a central role in the formation of the city's representation as moving images came to define the visual language and collective understanding of American culture. The variety of settings the region offered—beaches, desert, mountains, and the mainland—are encapsulated in the potent and abundant associations the palm provides through a visual shorthand, which the film and television industry could readily draw upon to increase production value. Add a dolly shot of a film's protagonist driving on any of the palm-lined streets in Hancock Park—say north on Windsor Boulevard, with its perfectly framed and unobstructed view of the Hollywood Sign—and suddenly your film is imbued with the ambient aura of Southern California.

The mystique provided by the palm has a useful range of meanings and can be utilized in one film to connote magic, and in another to convey menace. Putting aside their legibility and cultural associations, palms are also useful in a purely pragmatic sense for image-making. Their unique proportions mean that they can be discretely isolated with the tilt of a camera and intentionally situated in relation to other objects in the picture frame, as in John Baldessari's Kissing Series (1975) and Wrong (1966-68), or the "big W" in It's a Mad, Mad, Mad, Mad World (1963, dir. Stanley Kramer, United Artists). The mass and proportions of most other trees—say the Indian Laurel Figs (Ficus microcarpa) populating Downtown LA, or the squid-like veininess of the Moreton Bay Figs (Ficus macrophylla) punctuating the streets of the Hollywood

... Hills—preclude such photogenic reliability. Other trees simply lack the uniform regularity palms embody, a quality bestowed upon them as if they came from a factory or a prop house.

Most importantly and most obviously, the palm doesn't obstruct light. Unlike any other flora, it operates like a column propping up the sky rather than a canopy obstructing it. A palm can be photographed or filmed without getting in the way of the rich turquoise and celeste of the Southern California sky that invariably surrounds it (except during mornings of May Gray in late spring and June Gloom in early summer, when the marine layer of murky fog lingers until inevitably burning off in the early afternoon). But with the introduction of various invasive species, along with the broader ecological trauma of climate change, the city is now working to transition the landscape away from California palms, to flora perhaps less photogenic, but better suited for contemporary reality.

> “ Southern California is man-made, a gigantic improvisation. Virtually everything in the region has been imported: plants, flowers, shrubs, trees, people, water, electrical energy, and, to some extent, even the soils. [...] Even the weeds of the region are not native.”
>
> ▲ Carey McWilliams, Southern California: An Island on the Land (New York: Gibbs Smith, 1980), 13.

▲ **Rubberneckers**

▲ The ubiquitous clusters of satellite dishes that sprout up across domestic facades and low-rise rooftops throughout Southern California are so incredibly prosaic. Their matte gray surfaces seem resigned to collect dust and slowly bleach over years and years of exposure to the unrelenting sunlight.

And yet, imagining each individual dish as the endpoint to some invisible, gossamer tether, stretching out into the horizon to a lonely satellite spinning invisibly at its opposite end is so extraordinarily surreal! Is there an odd couple more dramatically in tension in the built landscape than the orbital

... satellite and its lowly dish? But then, aren't these types of odd couplings just what globalization is best at achieving? Our contemporary economic structures are specifically attuned to take such massive and abstract relationships and distill them down to a material reality so unremarkable as to barely merit our attention. A piece of fruit that is out-of-season yet available year-round at the produce stand, or the stacks of dirt cheap t-shirts at Target, which aren't inherently meaningful, but the immense engines of production and circulation of capital and resources that they represent is downright miraculous, if not perverse. At every moment of contemporary life, we're thrust into contact with forces and phenomena that so vastly mismatch us in scale. The points of contact that mediate the relationship are so inane: monotonous stacks of products bathed in fluorescent lighting, the embarrassing array of cereals, snacks, and sodas in aisle after aisle of store shelving, or a gaggle of aluminum parabolas staring dumbly at the California sun.

> “Finally I found something on the list, something vital: instant coffee. I held the red plastic container, one of the last three on the shelf, held it like the marvel that it was: the seeds inside the purple fruits of coffee plants had been harvested on Andean slopes and roasted and ground and soaked and then dehydrated at a factory in Medellín and vacuum-sealed and flown to JFK and then driven upstate in bulk to Pearl River for repackaging and then transported back by truck to the store where I now stood reading the label. It was as if the social relations that produced the object in my hand began to glow within it as they were threatened, stirred inside their packaging, lending it a certain aura—the majesty and murderous stupidity of that organization of time and space and fuel and labor becoming visible in the commodity itself now that planes were grounded and the highways were starting to close.”

▲ Ben Lerner, 10:04 (New York: Faber and Faber, Inc., 2014), 19.

▲ The digital turn in typesetting, more typically referred to as the advent of "desktop publishing," didn't simply reach its conclusion with the banality of family holiday newsletters and "Lost Dog" signs. Like movable type and the standardization of

… lettering and punctuation before it, every technological shift deprives us of some nuance or irreproducible quirk in the interest of convenience.

When people still wrote with pen and paper, they would simply make up their own punctuation marks to suit their mood! The implications for the built environment, how our neighborhoods and streetscapes look and feel, continue to reflect and synthesize the outsized influence of those moments in the 1980s and 1990s. During this turn to "desktop publishing," the palette of letterforms was locked-in, starting with the typeface **Chicago** in Apple systems, and expanding to include dreary storefront evocations set unimaginatively in Helvetica, Comic Sans, COPPERPLATE, and other charmless palettes of letterforms. **Cooper** is the only one with any redeeming character.

Typically the ludicrously inept are the only signs worth noticing. There is a dentist's office that we regularly pass in suburban New Jersey that has particularly noteworthy signage. They decided to duplicate the *Coca-Cola* lettering and ribbon in their storefront messaging. For some inscrutable reason, the phrase *Dental Implants* is written out in the instantly recognizable and intimately familiar loopy curves and swoops. Occasionally, while looking at historical photography, you might notice the tender care and character evident in some hand-painted advertising murals and other signs prior to rapid reproduction. ✍ With digital lettering in retail signage today, it seems like the only marks of distinction come from the most incomprehensible choices.

> "[…] I felt like a journeyman in a century gone by, so out of place that I should not have been surprised if a band of street urchins had come skipping after me or one of Middleton's householders had stepped out upon his threshold to tell me to be on my way. After all, every foot traveller incurs the suspicion of the locals, especially nowadays, and particularly if he does not fit the image of a local rambler."

▲ W.G. Sebald, The Rings of Saturn (New York: New Directions, 1999), 175.

✍ Note: Los Angeles Trade Technical College, just south of Downtown, offers an Associate in Arts Degree in Sign Graphics, with program courses such as Individual Lettering, Exterior Display Signs, and Fundamentals of Mural Painting. Delightfully, and perhaps inevitably, the college campus itself has become the display surface for the student's quirky efforts. Ever the selfless martyr, the building is offered-up in the interest of educational development (an unmistakable metaphor for the physical and emotional sacrifices that come with pedagogical practice, which any educator will instantly recognize). The segment of Flower Street that encompasses the revolving outdoor gallery of about two dozen large-scale murals is an endearing time capsule of class projects, with various aspirational messages of wholesome civic pride and …

… reimaginings of Angeleno identity. Around the corner, on Washington Boulevard, in a nondescript alley full of dumpsters and building systems machinery next to the college's culinary school, is the outdoor showcase of the hand-painted retail signage classes. A delightful buffet of storefront signs ("Luzecita's Panaderia," "Art Supplies," "Auto Body Shop," "Menotti's Coffee Shop," "Acosta's Carpet Cleaning," "General Store," etc.), all exhibited in sequence around the unglamorous semi-circle of the service alley. It's a sort of strip mall miniature, where the tender, loving care of each hand-painted crosshatch, offset letter, filigree, and drop shadow is evident at a cursory glance.

▲ **Adverse side effects**

Damage to the built environment often has a clarifying effect in its ability to expose the otherwise obscured interactions of various mechanical, electrical, structural, and material layers of a building. Such details, which are rarely available for scrutiny, make the everyday landscape of signs and structures slightly more relatable.

See: § 4, "*12'-1"" (pg. 98-99).
See: § 5, "Transparent drywall" (pg. 116-117).

Edifices and facades are often so precisely calibrated in order to confound and convince the public, and especially the nosy flâneur, to simply move along, that nothing worthy of scrutiny or curiosity is to be found here. What is striking about encountering some form of disassembly or ruination is the rendering of transparency, a sense of the obscure inner workings being made visible. It's like a surgical dissection: the satisfying simplicity of bone, ligament, and muscle made visible, but without the guilt of inflicting harm.

Any discomfort is replaced instead by the assurance of a productive and inevitable repair and replacement on the horizon—some insurance coverage has been invoked, and some competent repair team will be along shortly. For instance, a powerful windstorm struck the San Gabriel Valley in November of 2011, damaging or toppling over five-thousand trees and causing over $30 million in damage to public property. For weeks afterward, it was common to walk around Pasadena and other nearby towns and see, amidst the downed branches and power lines, the evidence of damage to the graphic landscape of the area: the shattered plastic orange globe and blue lettering of a 76 gas station sign, pieces of the namesake red and blue insignia of the Chevron sign, or the instantly recognizable remains of a yellow and red McDonald's sign. Inevitably, looking upward from the debris on the street, you would find yourself staring at an abstracted series of

... empty, aluminum frames with a few anonymous fluorescent white tubes still inside, like a rib cage. It's bizarre to encounter such stark evidence that this constellation of brands and icons seemingly holding consumer culture together is nothing more than colorful vacuum formed plastic and fluorescent light bulbs. Like being transfixed in some hallucinatory state, it was as if the coordinates of reality itself were no longer stable.

Eventually, the replacement coverings arrived and were installed. Almost as quickly as the storm struck, the memory of its destruction had been overwritten. The sense of urgency that hastened the replacement of the gas station signs seemed intent on removing any physical evidence that catastrophic weather events, once rare, were increasingly common. As climate change, and the concurrent unpredictability that it brings, becomes more and more a part of everyday life, these large storefront signs will either be built more sturdily—"hardened" to the increasingly harsh weather conditions—or they will continually be replaced at an exponentially rapid pace.

> " But the choice between the blue and the red pill is not really a choice between illusion and reality. Of course, Matrix is a machine for fictions, but these are fictions which already structure our reality. If you take away from our reality the symbolic fictions that regulate it, you lose reality itself. I want a third pill! So what is the third pill? Definitely not some kind of transcendental pill, which enables a fake fast food religious experience, but a pill that would enable me to perceive not the reality behind the illusion, but the reality in illusion itself. If something gets too traumatic, too violent, even too filled-in with enjoyment, it shatters the coordinates of our reality. We have to fictionalize it."
>
> ▲ Slavoj Žižek, The Pervert's Guide to Cinema (2006, dir. Sophie Fiennes, Microcinema International), 00:03:45.

▲ **Vinyl seam feels**

▲ There's a funny casualness around the potency of images in public spaces, and particularly in their depictions of the fragility of the human body.

An untold catalog of bodily violence confronts us on a daily basis: there's the alarmed flailing of the stick figure regularly seen as being crushed between two closing doors, depicted on warning signs near the doorways of commuter trains and subway cars. Or there's the sad cranial slump of the figure bludgeoned by a descending swing-arm gate, that moment of

… discomfort captured and recreated in warning signs in parking lots everywhere. In so many ways, the surprising convergence of the image and the surface evokes a startling sense of amusement rather than aversion, like the trivial distinction often made between depictions of violence and gore. Violence is a banal act, an unremarkable inevitability in our culture, and we're surrounded by evocations of it constantly. But gore and its outcome is somehow more gratuitous and irregular, more punitive and unnecessary, and is treated as less culturally acceptable in its depiction. 😐 The distinction seems exceptionally arbitrary.

😐 For a wonderfully exhaustive examination of this phenomenon and its connections to religion, eroticism, militarism, and authoritarianism, see: the filmography of Paul Verhoeven.

--- 🙃 ---

▲ **Face handles**

It's telling that a property developer would choose to cover a building with imagery of enormous, grinning white faces. Particularly when considering the overwhelming availability of stock photography, it's difficult not to feel confronted by an unsubtle message—one masked in the mundane language of promotion and marketing.

Without explicitly crossing any lines demarcated under the Fair Housing Act, we're assailed with an unmistakable bulletin, the subtext of which aims to reinforce the developer's blatantly racist preferences for potential tenants in the apartment complex. By masquerading the messaging as innocuous surface ephemera, we're meant to lower our guard, to imagine that such imagery—inserted into the street landscape of a historically Black neighborhood in South Central—is an arbitrary default: as if the photographic subjects depicted in this decorative treatment could just as easily be a field of flowers or idyllic rolling hillsides, like some pre-installed wallpaper. For all of the discourse about coffee shops, fences,[1] art galleries, and house paint color palettes as harbingers of gentrification,[2] it's striking how such blatant and insulting gestures, like filling the windows of vacant retail stores with photographs of idiotically celebratory white models, wouldn't also be prevalent in the conversation about pressures and inequities in neighborhood development and access to affordable housing.

> "Though some home-decorating magazines have experimented with human beings as photo props—'hired models in real homes' in the European editions of *Elle Décor*, and household servants in uniform in *House & Garden* ('we needed a figure for scale,' explained *H&G*'s editor)—the more common practice is to omit the humans and focus on the furniture, plants, and dogs."

[1] See: Jonny Coleman, "How These Wooden Fences Became a Symbol of Gentrification Across Los Angeles," *LAist*, May 4, 2016, web [https://laist.com/2016/05/04/wooden_slat_fences.php].

[2] See: Sofie Kodner, "San Francisco Is Turning Gray — One House at a Time," *KALW San Francisco Public Radio*, Sep. 10, 2019, web [https://www.kalw.org/post/san-francisco-turning-gray-one-house-time#stream/0].

63 ◀ Marjorie Garber, Sex and Real Estate: Why We Love Houses (New York: Pantheon Books, 2000), 17.

--- ❀ ---

▲ **Low-res cloud**

“ Posted 8 months ago
Discussion:

Why does pc still have low resolution clouds?

→ G-Double-D-Dilly: I play on ps4 pro and pc and it baffles me that the pc version still has these low res ugly blurry clouds. On ps4 pro they look great. What the hell? Shouldn't there be an option on pc to turn the clouds higher?

↳ Wolfhammer69: I've wondered about the clouds - they look like crap in VR, just these shimmery patches of blurry white crap. I'd love to fix them so they look at least half decent.

↳ tronaldmcdump: Volumetric setting is supposed to do this.

↳ G-Double-D-Dilly: Well it doesn't do anything to the clouds.. They are not even remotely close to looking as good [...]

↳ Jkthemc: I get lovely rolling clouds. How do they look on the console?

↳ G-Double-D-Dilly: It's the blurryness that is the problem.

↳ tronaldmcdump: Yeah mine look nothing like that [...]

↳ Jkthemc: That is pretty.

↳ Jkthemc: I think they are very authentic as opposed to photo pretty, and the animation is great. Obvioulsy the rest comes down to personal taste.

↳ G-Double-D-Dilly: Animations are not the issue, these are the same everywhere. I don't think anyone would think blurry low resolution clouds look better as their personal taste :P

↳ Jkthemc: I just don't agree that the other picture has “better looking clouds” That isn't what clouds actually look like close up.

↳ G-Double-D-Dilly: I don't know anyone who thinks these ugly pc clouds look even remotely good.

↳ Jkthemc: You do know someone. Me [...]

↳ G-Double-D-Dilly: They don't even fit the aestetic with the ground and buildings etc looking sharp contrasted with the blurry sky. It just doesn't work... But that's my opinion. You can be happy with the pc clouds, they still should add a slider for people who don't like them so blurry.

↳ Jkthemc: ... You are pointing to an optimised image made to look good, not a well rendered realistic image.

↳ G-Double-D-Dilly: I'm not going to argue with someone who claims lower resolution is better. Not even going to bother. You enjoy your blurry mess, i prefer not getting a headache because of the blur.

↳ Jkthemc: I am not saying that am I? This isn't a resolution issue this is a rendering issue. Clouds are soft and fluffy. They are misty up close. You clearly want clouds to look more like a computer game and that's fine...

↳ G-Double-D-Dilly: Sharpness has nothing to do with the fluffyness... They look like how they look in real life... Something can look fluffy and soft and still look sharp, that's how human vision works [...] Make all excuses you want but i don't believe you yourself believe a word you are saying. I think you just make excuses to fool yourself because you don't have access to the good looking clouds...

↳ Jkthemc: You are not convincing me. Like I said this is a taste issue... they know people think of clouds as how they look from the ground. That picture is a choice made by them to make it look pretty. It does indeed look pretty. Not how I want clouds to look in my game but you have that option...

↳ G-Double-D-Dilly: Everything you just said is bs. Go bother someone else.

↳ Jkthemc: I also haven't tinkered for long beacause I personally don't want my clouds to look different anyway.

↳ G-Double-D-Dilly: Looks like garbage to be honest... thats why they implemented the true cloud tech... Also clouds don't look like that in real life, i'm looking at the sky right now and they are sharp, fluffy and good looking [...]"

▲ G-Double-D-Dilly, "Why does pc still have low resolution clouds?" Reddit r/NoMansSky, Feb. 25, 2020 [https://www.reddit.com/r/NoMansSkyTheGame/comments/f98lno/why_does_pc_still_have_low_resolution_clouds/fiq03jy/].

--- 💻 ---

▲ **Easy fast neon install**

▲ The structural delicacy of a neon sign still occasionally found hanging in some store windows, the skeletal narrowness of its glowing glass tracery and the vascular interconnectedness of

… its wires and tubes often feels amusingly discordant with the tone of mundane, reliable consumer messaging that it's called upon to convey.

Equally amusing is the responsibility granted to a store employee to control that messaging; particularly in the middle of the night in the suburbs, where there seems to be less discipline with such formalities. There's something delightfully subversive about driving around and seeing strip mall storefront after strip mall storefront, interiors vacant, dark, and still, the windows adorned with the cavalier glowing assurance of red letters snugly situated inside of a blue oval: **OPEN**. This sense of delight can be easily simulated by visiting a store signage wholesaler * (provided, of course, that they're **OPEN**), and taking in the visual wonderment of an entire product display wall completely covered in different varieties of **OPEN** signs, each blinking and flashing to its own accord. It's utterly euphoric! One suspects that the effect could be produced with almost any object or component of the retail landscape: just isolate and duplicate the object ad infinitum and enjoy.

* See: Any number of store signage wholesalers located in Downtown Los Angeles; for an especially delightful exemplar, visit Kingstar Products, Inc. on 3rd Street.

> “ The paradoxes of this problem of the proliferation of images are most clearly articulated in pop art, which has taken its place within the abstract space of mass culture and the mass spectacle at the same time that it has usurped the space of public sculpture. The Oldenburgs that dot the urban landscapes of Chicago and Philadelphia are the legendary giants, the topographical mascots, of those cities. They are relatives of other forms of the architecture-of-the-above, particularly the billboard and the neon sign, those forms which are all facade. And they are representations of mechanical reproduction arrested into authenticity by being ‘original objects.’”

▲ Susan Stewart, <u>On Longing: Narratives of the Miniature, the Gigantic, the Souvenir, the Collection</u> (Durham, NC: Duke University Press, 1993), 92.

- - - - - -

Stucco spolia

Stucco gets a bad rap. Or rather, and perhaps worse, it doesn't really get any rap at all.

... Easily the most common material choice for exterior finishes on buildings in Los Angeles, its noisy uniformity—like the black-and-white static fuzz on an old television set—provides predictable regularity through inconsistency. Unlike bricks or siding, the visual demands of patterning are less important with stucco, whether in the slightly more antiquated and fussy arcs of hand-troweled applications found on older bungalows in Hollywood, or the more expedient sprayed-on nubby applications to apartment buildings throughout the region. While it's been used in various forms since at least the 1st century, it hasn't necessarily been defined as a specific material, but more as a range of recipes with similar functional and formal outcomes. Its unrelenting sameness is an easy target of derision: a building surface lacking in character. Stucco is a continuous, totalizing material. Like carpet, it adds blurriness to a surface, making proportional relationships and obscene contrasts of scale less apparent. It conveys a sense of unflappable disregard for the surface conditions as it hides everything beneath it.

These qualities are nicely suited for the particularities of Los Angeles, a city that is uniquely in a state of constant rewriting and reconfiguration. On a walk a few years ago in South Pasadena, we noticed a shocking and concerning viral spread on dozens of cacti and succulents in front of a self-storage facility. They seemed to be afflicted with a mysterious, lumpy, beige mold, but on closer inspection, it became clear that a contractor had been overly zealous with the spray-on stucco application. They had covered the exterior wall, along with the prickly pears, jades, and yuccas. Ever resilient, the desert flora simply went on thriving, lapping up the sunshine of the southern exposure, albeit slightly diminished in those portions that had been stuccoed and turned into the stable, unchanging surface of the built environment.

“ The blp really was a sort of conceptual high note, in terms of making something that was nothing more than a signal for you to see other things.”

▲ Whitney Museum of American Art, “Richard Artschwager, blps, 1967-,” YouTube, Nov. 20, 2012, web [https://www.youtube.com/watch?v=ELIo2zY2AQw] 1:54.

--- ≈ ---

▲ **Uncanny valley**

The unending charm of Masahiro Mori's term is in the poetically evocative tint it casts on what could have otherwise been an obtuse and dispassionate observation. Pointing out the varying degree of creepiness in puppets, manequins, robots, building facades, and other creations that reproduce human facial expressions, postures, and gestures isn't especially novel.

But to articulate it with a level of precision and terminology so strikingly expressing both an emotion and a spatial condition elevates the label and imbeds it indelibly in the imagination; it's a term that can't be unheard or unremembered.

Rather than simply describing the relationships of two values on a coordinate plane (the "valley" refers to a graph visualizing the phenomenon, which accompanies Mori's article), it brings to mind a haunting and hazy emotion tied to some specific destination and experience.

The Uncanny Valley sounds like a setting torn directly from the fabric of a dream or a distant memory. It lets the mind wander, stumbling upon the eponymous Valley on a map. Like the Pine Barrens or the Badlands, it's a place that evokes an emotion purely through the invocation of its name. The staying power and provocative potential of the term leads one to imagine an entire expanded category of sensations or impressions in which representation and interactive overlay have callously wandered too close to the boundary that neatly divides the real from the unreal, or the living from the inanimate. We might more appropriately start to describe ourselves as having momentarily tumbled into the Uncanny Valley when we sleepily swipe-left on a glossy portrait in a magazine, or drunkenly double-tap a sunset viewed through a window.

\- - - - - -

See: Masahiro Mori, "The Uncanny Valley," Energy, Vol. 7, No. 4 (1970), 33-35.

See: Jorge Luis Borges, "Of Exactitude in Science," A Universal History of Infamy, trans. Norman Thomas di Giovanni (New York: E.P. Dutton & Co., Inc., 1970), 141.

▲ **Utility palm**

▲ There's a lovely formal duality between the palm tree and the utility pole. The latter is defined by the sturdy, confident rigidity of its horizontal projections, authoritative and objective like Leonardo's Vitruvian Man, and the former defined by the saggy casualness of its fanned and feathered leaves.

... While it's tempting to associate the palm's graphic potency, with those leafy Corinthian projections, its iconic quality can also be credited to the fuzzy brown collar just below the green projection of the fronds. Like the diagrammatic device employed in many historical engravings of the classical orders, which comically collapses entablatures and capitals onto bases with only minimal articulation of column shaft or fluting in between, it's easy to think of the iconic California palm as a composition of three basic pieces: crown, collar, and trunk.

Since so much of contemporary visual culture has been defined through depictions of Los Angeles (television, film, video games, music videos, etc.), the city, the contours of its landscape and the characteristics of its flora becomes a sort of baseline for evaluating one's life in America. If it was simply an accident of climate and culture that Los Angeles became the filmic capital of the Western world—moderate temperatures plus abundant sunlight plus ready accessibility to lots of varieties of nearby landscapes—then perhaps it's also merely coincidental that palm trees and cacti both share in common the iconic reproducibility, recognizability, and graphic simplicity of a logo. The California palm and the Saguaro cactus (although not native to Los Angeles, but certainly a prevalent import) are icons. Sure, a coniferous or deciduous tree is recognizable as a profile or a graphic symbol, but not to the extent that it can carry with it the associations and immediate legibility as compared to an explosion of palm fronds swaying lazily in the breeze.

The accumulation of dried and desiccated old leaves in vertical sequence down the palm's trunk becomes a record of passing time. As such, palms can be thought of as sensors—maybe a sort of "broken windows theory" for the natural environment—that provide an insight into the self-image and extents of maintenance and aspiration for a neighborhood. The campuses of the University of California, Los Angeles and the University of Southern California, for instance, are largely devoid of any shaggy brown fronds. The showiness of more affluent neighborhoods, like Brentwood and Beverly Hills, gives rise to a bizarrely scrupulous manicuring of the palms, in which only two of the youngest, pertest leaflets at the very top of the crown will be permitted to remain, standing utterly vertical and alone; the older, more horizontally reclined fronds are removed entirely (the metaphorical implications are too cloyingly obvious to even mention).

For one example among many, see: Claude Perrault, Ordonnance for the Five Kinds of Columns After the Method of the Ancients (United States: Getty Center for the History of Art and the Humanities, 1993) 141.

... Meanwhile, if you venture in the opposite direction, away from the coast and inland to the light-industrialized expanses southeast of Downtown, you're more likely to find palms, ironically, in their more natural, unmanicured state. For instance, you might occasionally see a denser, fully fronded palm punctuating mega-block after mega-block in the euphoric and otherworldly city of Vernon (population 112), where enormous warehouses seem to repeat algorithmically, extending off into infinity, like some primitive mid-1990s computer modeling simulation,✯ the sequence interrupted only by the occasional, lowly, disregarded palm.

✯ See: § 5, "Riverbend access door" (pg. 130-132).

And finally, but certainly leaving the most lasting impression in the catalog of encounters with palms that one can undergo in Los Angeles, is the sight of a palm crown on fire. A spectacle usually reserved for the Fourth of July or New Year's Eve, one can't help but feel some mournful, elegiac meaning in the blackened and smoldering fronds of an unfortunate palm, which had its own slow and steady upward trajectory interrupted by the coinciding path of an oncoming bottle rocket.

> “ The palms were beautiful trees in their way, especially as part of a quartet, but there is an intrinsic scrawniness to the palm, which grows like a flaring match, with a little fizzle of green at the top. It is doing only what is absolutely necessary to do to be a tree; and it has big, coarse leaves—intemperate leaves—and the bark shows its years on the outside, so that the tree has no secrets: it doesn't have to be cut down before you can date its birth."
>
> ▲ Nicholson Baker, A Box of Matches (New York: Random House, 2003), 21-22.

- - - (- - -

§ 3 - There are many ways to arrive at a **compromise**: squishing, squeezing, chopping, cropping, overlapping, underlapping, giving in, or just giving up. But the stubbornness of architectural forms in the face of building codes, regulations, material constraints, and the limitations of physics often requires relinquishing some degree of agency and instead, conceding to simply make-do.

▲ **Obstructed view**

▲ The term “building code” always seems to fall short of the imaginative promise its double-meaning suggests.

The idea of a “code,” or an attendant “source code,” for buildings—like a recipe or a magical incantation for bringing structures into the world—is exciting because it suggests there’s a consensus starting point for generating built form. Maybe this is why SketchUp ❐ is so enticing; in its blithely simple presentation of shapes and operations, the software seems to insist that all buildings really do just start out as boxes. Whether an ancient ruin, a venerable temple, or a disregarded strip mall, SketchUp’s totalizing approach to form regards them all equally, as flat planes joined together at their edges. Fussy little articulations like cupolas or trim, symbols or

... signage, are the only aspects that distinguish one from the other—some extraneous details, tacked-on, and extruded-out from the initial form. Unfortunately, the true "source code" for the built environment can't really be found by looking through building codes or other municipal regulations, but is disseminated in the hypnotic din of wall-to-wall programming blocks of home renovation shows cramming the schedules of various network and cable television stations such as A&E, Bravo, HGTV, and TLC. These shows are apparently innocuous enough to enjoy a ubiquitous status as the default channel selection on televisions in every single waiting room, building lobby, and gym across the country, and almost always with the audio muted. This category of entertainment—ostensibly aimed at aspiring fixers, flippers, and D.I.Y.ers—seems carefully tailored to be completely ignored. The first half of each episode dwells on the spectacle of the mess, the requisite "before" shots, inviting the audience—many of whom may find themselves in environs remarkably similar to the interiors depicted—to ascend to the privileged status of bemused critic, simultaneously pitying the episode's targeted living space, while also endowed with the unwavering inspiration and vision that demolition and rehabilitation can supposedly bring to all interiors.

See: § 1, "Extrusions by SketchUp" (pg. 36–37).

See: Fix This Yard, Flip This House, Flip Wars, Flipping Boston, Flipping Vegas, Home.Made., Operation Build, Sell This House!, Vacation Rental Potential, Working the Room, and Zombie House Flipping.

See: Backyard Envy, Best Room Wins, Buying It Blind, Flipping Exes, Flipping Out, Get a Room with Carson & Thom, Interior Therapy with Jeff Lewis, and Million Dollar Decorators.

The solutions proffered in each show are remarkably repetitive. Once the invasive diagnosis is delivered, a frenzied rush of semi-coherent video editing—a shot of a sledgehammer rupturing through plaster, a cabinet being pried off a wall, and a section of countertop callously tossed onto a debris pile—gives way to the transcendent bliss of the renovated "after," accompanied by a satisfying musical sting. A cursory viewing of any of these shows reveals the recurring pattern for all of their restorative "solutions": paint most of the surfaces gray-blue or dark gray, add some white trim for contrast, knock down some walls for an "open concept" plan, and mount some "distressed" wood panels for an accent. Then repeat.

While we tend to think of neighborhoods and their surrounding communities as constituted through an incredibly complex set of interrelationships and unquantifiable attributes, the primary function of the real estate market is to evaluate and assign value to these otherwise elusive characteristics.

See: Curb Appeal, Design on a Dime, Designed to Sell, Extreme Makeover: Home Edition, Fixer Upper, Flip or Flop, Good Bones, Love It or List It, Property Brothers, Rehab Addict, and Rustic Rehab.

See: Building Off the Grid, Buying Naked, Extreme Homes, Hidden Money Makeover, Maine Cabin Masters, My First Home, Nate & Jeremiah by Design, Playhouse Masters, Say Yes to the Address, Texas Flip and Move, Trading Spaces, and While You Were Out.

… Metrics like school rankings, property value trends, and walkability scores are now requisite analytics in the complex data sheets of statistics comprising a home sale listing today. But it's largely left to the boilerplate, adjective-laden blathering of the written listing description, which usually seems to have been laboriously authored by the listing agent, to diplomatically convey the subtext. These paragraphs provide a surprisingly rich anthropological cross-section for exploring consumer culture's relationships with built form. Of course, terms like "fixer-upper" and "cozy" seem to have entered the broader vernacular through their usefulness for positively describing undesirable characteristics of apartments and houses for sale or rent. Ultimately, it's nice to consider that almost every house has had some small piece of prose written in its honor. Otherwise, qualities like views, vistas, and scenery surrounding a home are quantified through property assessments, but also in the meandering conversation that inevitably takes place between prospective occupants and a real estate agent during an open house or a showing.

Higher floors in condo buildings afford more sweeping, dramatic, unobstructed, and desirable views. There's a proportional relationship between cost and floor number: the higher the floor, the higher the price tag. This is not inseparable from the three most important rules in real estate: "Location, Location, Location." A view directly impeded by an egress stairway in an apartment building really shifts the meaning of a "desirable view." Perhaps the unique ability to keep tabs on the comings and goings of one's neighbors—a de facto enlistment as the neighborhood watch—is as valuable as a dramatically sweeping panoramic view of the city. A window directly onto the main staircase is a passive, analog version of the NextDoor app, mounted permanently to your living room wall: a constantly streaming, nosy viewport into every other resident's life. Don't so many popular television crime procedurals rely on the hearsay of some building resident, hesitantly providing the decisive tip, in just such a compromised position?

--- $ ---

▲ **IRL VR**

▲ Living in an era in which online life is increasingly, beguilingly entangled with offline life, it's striking how extensive the intrusion of virtual and augmented experiences have become around sites of tourism and historic preservation.

The careful and painstaking labor of protecting antiquities has always been in an uncomfortable relationship with the destructive, consumptive impulses

… of the touristic industry. (Not long ago, the two practices were basically indistinguishable—browsing back through historical accounts, it's difficult to differentiate between the callous romping and stomping mentality of early archaeologists, and the "ugly tourist" stereotype of contemporary casual global vacationing culture). It's increasingly common to encounter augmented reality tours and other "immersive experiences" embedded within historical sites as interpretive tools for visitors, or popping-up around the periphery in storefronts adjacent to the requisite t-shirt vendors and gift shops. Of course, this phenomenon begs the question: how tenuous is the connection between proximity and relevance? If visitors are willing to forgo the IRL historic site in favor of a high-definition virtual reality headset, then why travel at all?

The devastation wrought on brick and mortar retail by the Internet, and Amazon specifically, is being met more and more with creative reappropriation by purveyors of "experiences." Vacant storefronts in once-thriving suburban malls and on historically bustling commercial main streets across the country are transforming into an array of offerings that seek to expand the horizon of reality and routine life: escape rooms, marijuana dispensaries, and augmented or virtual experiences. Perhaps a bit too on-the-nose, many of these eerily abandoned intersections of American commerce and culture are now hosting VR zombie hunting forays. After a visit to Richard Neutra's Garden Grove Community Church (1962) and Gin D. Wong's Crean Tower and Mary Hood Chapel (1990), while wandering the hinter-regions of the nearby Outlets of Orange shopping mall, it only seems appropriate that the breathless promotional messaging of a vinyl wrap storefront display would invite a reckoning with the escapist implications of "virtual" reality. With its extreme proximity to Disneyland, the City of Orange—and Orange County in general—are already strikingly virtual environments. It only seems appropriate that an enterprise offering temporary enlistment in zombie warfare should be situated seamlessly between a Banana Republic outlet store and a Starbucks.

Zombie militarism somehow makes sense in a place like Orange County, but why not among the antiquity and ruins of ancient Rome as well? Since virtual spaces seem to invite such wanton flattening of context and propriety, why not offer visitors the opportunity to liberate Nero's palatial Golden Dome from marauding zombies, aliens, or any other flavor of incursion? And for that matter, why not do so from the comfort and convenience of the Outlets of Orange shopping mall?

For instance, guided tours of the Domus Aurea in Rome added an obligatory virtual reality component around 2017. A few months later, nighttime audio-visual programs were offered at both the Fora of Augustus and Caesar, featuring massive projection mapped visuals supplemented by straightforward explanations of the current ruins, as well as dramatic depictions of historic catastrophes and day-to-day life during antiquity in the forum, including narration in six different languages, dramatic musical cues, and sound effects.

See: § 8, "Dental retainer door handle" (pg. 191-192).

> “This synchrony of street and theater was not coincidental but represented the double role of urban space and theatrical space in humanistic culture; even as the public realm of the street took on the functions of the theater of daily life—the city as a stage for the social action within its protecting walls—so did the theater retain its place as the mnemonic device par excellence the ideal depiction of the world. The building of the streets inside the theater brought the space of the real into the domain of the ideal, the memory of the one allowing the observation and perhaps the critique of the other.”
>
> ▲ Anthony Vidler, The Scenes of the Street and Other Essays (New York City: The Monacelli Press, 2011), 18.

◀ User-interface designers and architects share more in common than one might imagine.

Both work through the depiction of a “program,” a set of instructions that organize potential outcomes and experiences. And the distance between the two fields collapses even further when we arrive at a building labeled as a “virtual museum.” This new category suggests the interior could be imagined as a device or merely an operating system that serves as a software environment for the program—crashing both architecture and interface together.

This conflation of “programs” is made possible by the flexibility of the term. Etymologically speaking, “program” moves seamlessly from the public realm to the classical concert performance to television and radio broadcasts to the computer, and at some pivotal moment along the way, to architecture.

This semantic overlap in the terminology of theater, computer programming, and architecture materializes in the Virtual Archaeological Museum of Ercolano, located near the site of the ancient Italian town on the Gulf of Naples destroyed in the aftermath of the infamous Mount Vesuvius eruption in 79 CE. Adopting slogans such as “The Most Advanced Museum Ever,” “The Past Seen with the Eyes of the Future,” “Technology at the Service of the Culture,” “The Eruption of Vesuvius in 5D,” and “History Will Never Seem the Same,” this is a museum as

... a technological spectacle of destruction, by way of an architectural tour. It should be noted one must be present, in-person, physically inhabiting the museum in order to engage with the entirely technologically mediated and completely virtual experiences it has to offer.

--- ---

▲ **Handrail vistas**

◂ There are precious few interior details and building elements—such as handrails, light switches, electrical outlets, and doorknobs—for which the conventions of their placement are so narrowly prescribed that even the slightest deviation from the norm can feel downright scandalous.

This is particularly true when it comes to vertical dimensions: light switches are mounted 48 inches from the ground, protective guard rails are 42 inches tall, doorknobs are 36 inches from the bottom of the door, and electrical outlets are 12 inches from the finished floor. This predictability fosters an intensely strong sense of personal betrayal when any aberrations are encountered, particularly because these objects are points of regular bodily contact with the built environment. The intimate immediacy of muscle memory and arm length creates a sense of personal trust and dependency. We all know the unique feeling of sullen disappointment caused by a poorly placed light switch—the sense of ineffectual embarrassment we feel after groping idiotically against an unresponsive section of plaster or drywall in a dark room, the paranoia in being confronted by this subterfuge of functional artifacts, our command and control of the environment destabilized. The conventions and standards dictating the placement of these touch-points produce a rote expectation of the world around us, such that environments can seem alienating when these rules are not respected.

I distinctly recall the sense of confusion caused by a doorbell on a neighboring house from my childhood. It seemed to be mounted peculiarly low, even to my miniaturized self. I was convinced the original owners must have been shorter than average. This seemed like the most obvious explanation. In retrospect, it's entirely possible it was just an arbitrary choice made during a do-it-yourself install: a Weekend Warrior shrugging their shoulders and drilling a hole in the door trim at about waist height. Most of the housing stock in the area had gone up in quick succession to accommodate post-war suburbanization and the Baby Boom soon to follow. Built in

… the 1950s and 1960s, the suburb was characterized by single-family homes punctuated by comparatively stately Victorian farmhouses dating back to the turn of the century—slightly legible imprints on the landscape from the village's not-too-distant agrarian past. The first wave of suburban settlers, however, were steadily aging-out by the early 1990s. Thinking back, this errant doorbell must have been placed about level with the door handle itself, which seems intuitive enough if you've never thought too deeply about common mounting heights for doorbells. It's strange that doorbell buttons followed the conventions of light switches in their suggested mounting height (generally 48 inches from the ground), rather than the height of the "analog" technology that they replaced, the door knocker, which is almost always mounted at something closer to eye-level (56 inches). As the trend of making every single domestic device "smart" and invasive continues apace, the doorbell is an obvious locus of ubiquitous surveillance, capture, and sharing. The inexorable creep of networked devices will soon engulf every doorbell button, electrical outlet, light switch, thermostat, and doorknob around us. As such, the demands of networked video cameras, passive infrared motion detectors, and noise sensors will only serve to cement these placement conventions more and more. ●

● For instance: the troubleshooting documentation available online for the Video Doorbell by Ring, Inc. (previously Bot Home Automation, Inc.) explains that, although many customers assume they should mount the product to align with average face height, in fact, the more convention doorbell mounting height of 48 inches is the ideal positioning to maximize the field of view and detection calibration for the litany of networked sensors and recording devices comprising their home surveillance product.

> "§ 3.6.1.2 The Architect shall advise and consult with the Owner during the Construction Phase Services. The Architect shall have authority to act on behalf of the Owner only to the extent provided in this Agreement. The Architect shall not have control over, charge of, or responsibility for the construction means, methods, techniques, sequences or procedures, or for safety precautions and programs in connection with the Work, nor shall the Architect be responsible for the Contractor's failure to perform the Work in accordance with the requirements of the Contract Documents. The Architect shall be responsible for the Architect's negligent acts or omissions, but shall not have control over or charge of, and shall not be responsible for, acts or omissions of the Contractor or of any other persons or entities performing portions of the Work."

▲ The American Institute of Architects, "AIA Document B101 – 2017 Standard Form of Agreement Between Owner and Architect."

- - - - - -

▲ **Arch downsizing**

There's something about an arch within an arch that feels ever so slightly discomforting to behold.

Like when a conversation turns to a friend or an acquaintance who is afflicted with some incredibly specific phobia, one can't help but try to muster a bit of empathetic agitation, even if that specific anxiety described isn't one that actually preoccupies us. As a child, I remember the marble-mouth pronunciations and polysyllabic constructions of various phobias were a predictably tedious and reoccurring trivia topic. It seemed like the back sides of cereal boxes and precocious classmates were often disappointingly eager to quiz or recite some list of anomalous conditions at the slightest provocation. This is probably because the construction of the terminology is so predictable and rewards a pretentiously cursory knowledge of Greek roots and various mythologies (for example, connecting the weaver Arachne to arachnophobia).

In the realm of public space, agoraphobia has such a moody, atmospheric quality. I'm never quite sure if it's describing the fear of a vast, yawning, deserted agora—an eerily abandoned public space, like the set pieces that so often punctuate zombie or post-apocalyptic survival films—or if it's the public itself causing the discomfort, with masses of people strolling, mingling, shuffling, loitering, roughhousing, peddling, and pestering. Otherwise, the terms megalophobia or batophobia are variously used to describe irrational and persistent fears of being near or inside of extremely large or tall objects, like skyscrapers. Gephyrophobia, the fear of bridges and tunnels, might be slightly appropriate for the nested arch situation.

But trypophobia seems to uniquely address our current cultural moment: a reaction to clusters of voids or groupings of holes. Described by a self-assertive group on Facebook, this particular phobia has yet to gain professional recognition in clinical journals; it's hard not to see this phenomenon as a direct response to the ubiquity online of imagery produced through neural network processes. The outcome of such visualizations, which circulate through popular memes and social media feeds, often take on a slippery, amorphous quality of showing unidentifiable shapes folding and clustering, and inevitably seeming to resolve into barely recognizable depictions of masses of human anatomy: globs of pores, ears, or eyes. The hideous mutations and nightmarish creatures increasingly manifest through outputting the algorithmic "dreams" of artificial intelligence are a sort of arch-within-an-arch—a vision that leaves us with a vague but persistent

See: In particular, 28 Days Later (2002, dir. Danny Boyle, DNA Films/UK Film Council).

See: Alexander Mordvintsev, "DeepDream," Google, Inc., 2015, software.

... sense of strange repetition and indifference to functional redundancy. In this case, the uncomfortable sense of massing and duplication results from the practicalities of standardized consumer products and specified dimensions of off-the-shelf building parts (the smaller arch corresponds to the size of manufactured exterior doors, a regularized width of about 36 inches).

--- ⌛ ---

▲ **Splitting the difference**

Doors perform the role of brutally indifferent, repressive enforcers of edge conditions just as often as they play the role of magnanimous moderators between two states.

Grids can have a similar effect on surfaces—not so much in mediating, but as a tactic to smooth over differences, to level playing fields, to impose an ordered, idealized, regulated system, and at the same time, to call out very clearly and isolate a deviant condition. Conflicts often arise between two regulatory systems: one that is usually abstract (the grid) and one that engages more at the scale of the body (the door). Like a grid, doors belong to a rigorously defined set of dimensions that could be understood as derived from the repeated exercise of applying grids to bodies. As ever, cinematic instances of slapstick, pratfalls, and other unexpected physical manipulation more broadly, provide some of the most potent visual discourse between bodies and regulatory systems: Buster Keaton miraculously slipping through a window frame, Jacques Tati reckoning with cubicles and floor tiles in an ultramodern Paris, or Leslie Nielsen visibly walking around the scenery flats of interior offices. In certain instances, the door, which exists on an edge and mediates between two different states by allowing passage, comes into conflict with the grid, which mediates by removing difference through abstraction. But the most interesting things always happen at the edges.

> "Besides, interesting things happen along borders—transitions—not in the middle where everything is the same."
>
> Neal Stephenson, Snow Crash (New York: Bantam Spectra, 1992), 122.

See: Da Vinci and Le Corbusier.

See: Steamboat Bill, Jr. (1928, dir. Charles Reisner, Buster Keaton Productions).

See: Playtime (1967, dir. Jacques Tati, Specta Films).

See: The Naked Gun: From the Files of Police Squad! (1988, dir. David Zucker, Paramount Pictures).

The Getty Museum in Los Angeles typifies a more general phenomenon found throughout the city in which there seems to be a lack of consensus among buildings regarding which direction to "face."

Beginning in the early 1960s and 1970s, department stores, especially in Los Angeles, began to "face" the parking lot instead of the street, privileging those who arrived by car rather than by foot. The Getty is similar, in that it creates a "face" for visitors disembarking from the tram (delivering you to the site from the parking structure down the hill), as well as presenting a "face" to those driving north on the 405. Rather than presenting a clear front to the individual patron, it subsumes them within an all-encompassing 30-inch-by-30-inch grid, placing each visitor within the historical lineage of bodies being put on grids (and vice versa) to idealize or measure them. Although the Getty might be attempting to deploy doors without having to imply a "face," when the grid and the door overlap in asynchrony an artifact of this incongruity is produced.

See, in particular: the dramatic frontage onto Olympic Boulevard at Boyle Avenue of George Nimmons's Sears, Roebuck & Company Mail Order Building (1927) in Boyle Heights. Most of the massive facility was a retail distribution center until 1992, which accounts for the strange sense of confusion it suffers regarding which way to "face." The grand staircase of the three-story street-facing entrance seems resolutely an artifact of the 1930s in its willingness to privilege, and even elevate, the laborers required to carry out the distribution that made the mail order catalogue distributor famous. By comparison, the consumer-facing retail frontage on the building's east side feels downright timid, with its tedious expanse of parking lot and matter-of-fact lettering above the doors reading: "RETAIL ENTRANCE."

> "The streets in my city are a fraction of a larger grid, anchored to one in Los Angeles. That grid was laid out in September 1781. [...] The Los Angeles grid is a copy of one carried from Mexico City to an anonymous stretch of river bank by Colonel Felipe de Neve, governor of California. [...] The grid the Spanish colonel carried to the nonexistent Los Angeles in 1781 originally came from a book in the Archive of the Indies in Seville. The book prescribed the exact orientation of the streets, the houses, and the public places for all the colonial settlements in the Spanish Americas. [...] That grid came from God."
>
> D.J. Waldie, Holy Land: A Suburban Memoir (New York: W. W. Norton Company, 2005), 22.

- - - - - -

▲ **Community beautification**

The Office of Community Beautification is responsible for graffiti removal in Los Angeles. A subsection of the city's Department of Public Works, the office contracts enough painting in one year to cover each letter of the Hollywood Sign with paint about 9 inches thick—approximately 1,800 coats—rolled out across each face of the four-story tall letters.

For an earlier and extended version of this text, see: Ian Besler, "June Gloom Gray: Who Chooses the Paint Color for Graffiti Abatement in Los Angeles?" Medium, Mar. 2015, web [https://medium.com/re-form/june-gloom-gray-967ab5917396].

Since the Office's internal statistics take into account the three common methods of graffiti removal (painting, chemical washing, and pressure blasting), this hypothetical figure is probably a bit conservative. But if half of the graffiti removal the Office oversees is accomplished through painting, then we're talking about enough cumulative pigment to completely cover two square miles of the city's surfaces over the 15-year period for which statistics are available; two square miles of stucco, brick, concrete, cinder block, plywood, metal, and more. Hundreds of thousands of surfaces have been abstracted to a manufactured color of paint, defaced, then brought back as if through the efforts of Hollywood set builders, their material fidelity slightly reduced, but close enough to pass. The scale of this effort is staggering, and the complexity of it is made trickier by the fact that the work aspires for invisibility. If any color of paint would suffice, or if any method of removal would do, it might be a simpler task. But community beautification, done as a concerted effort, demands a level of scrutiny with the built environment few of us will ever experience.

The online graffiti abatement request portal, accessed at either the Los Angeles County Public Works website or the City of Los Angeles MyLA311 website, is a means for anyone with access to a computer to assert control over the ephemeral qualities of architecture and space around them. Walking, cycling, using public transit, mobile mapping applications, or driving through Los Angeles, one is left with the impression that, no matter our differences, at least we all seem to have arrived at some tacit agreement: concrete is gray, stucco is beige, tree trunks are brown, and bricks are red.

▲ **Lobby transplants**

▲ Potted plants have held an iconic, if not infamous, role in interior corporate environments since the 1960s when the "office landscape," largely developed in post-war Germany and

... popularized across Europe, started to gain favor as a layout strategy in the United States.

Major companies of the time adopted the emerging ideal of innovative, progressive, non-hierarchical interior organization—such as IBM, Eastman Kodak, and DuPont—and commissioned new corporate headquarters and office plans with minimal formal distinctions between functions and purposes. Because this type of plan, known as office landscape, eschewed the ordered, repetitive tedium of discrete offices and narrow hallways in favor of openness, these groupings of ficus, philodendron, fiddle-leaf, palms, and ferns were strategically put to work. Placed in stands or rows to subtly punctuate and regulate space, at the same time, plant life presented a symbol of organic, holistic, and flexible organization. Their purpose in the workspace is both functional and poetic, utilitarian and decorative, economical and nurturing. Studies have validated the benefits of plants for psychologically restorative impacts. They reduce stress, enliven the humdrum appearance of the modern workplace, increase office productivity, improve indoor air quality, and provide an overall sense of well-being.

Perhaps they serve as an extremely subtle "sentinel species," similar in function to the idiomatic canary in the coal mine, but on a more subconscious level; could any given office environment really be so toxic (whether figuratively or literally) if a bunch of potted ferns thrive there? The vibrant green and nubile leafy robustness of any given floral species seems to insist that its surroundings are nurturing and supportive of life. Considering the entire range of possible decorative options for an office, it's also worth evaluating plants from a more pragmatic perspective: they are simply large, colorful, self-explanatory objects. They are reasonably priced and generally uncontroversial. Sculptures and paintings have the nasty side affect of eliciting unanticipated associations in a viewer's mind, whether symbolic, cultural, or political. ⊠ While fine art installed throughout an office can be a potent indicator of taste and cultural participation on behalf of the company, it can also suggest allegiances and associations that a major corporation might want to avoid. But try to name a controversial plant. Of course, the corpse flower ✲ or Venus flytrap jump to mind as potentially unsavory office companions. But granting those, and any other carnivorous and carrion plant examples, the exception proves the rule.

--- ✿ ---

⊠ See, for instance: Steve Lopez, "LAPD Gets 'Cow Splat' for Art," Los Angeles Times, Oct. 21, 2009, web [https://www.latimes.com/archives/la-xpm-2009-oct-21-me-lopez21-story.html].

✲ See: "Amorphophallus titanum," Wikipedia, web, n.d. [https://en.wikipedia.org/wiki/Amorphophallus_titanum].

▲ **Multipurpose building**

▲ Along with jetpacks, hoverboards, and flying cars, the possibility of "flex spaces" and meaningfully adaptable architecture represents just another episode in an ongoing series of betrayals inflicted upon our consensus imagined future by the technologists, industrialists, planners, and developers

… responsible for contemporary culture. This sense of disappointment still reverberates from the 1970s, in the example of the Pompidou Centre.

The recently completed Bloomberg Building, and adjoining McCourt, known colloquially as "The Shed" (2019) constitute a rolling, expandable portion of performance hall space for the eponymous arts organization in Midtown Manhattan. Designed by Diller Scofidio + Renfro, the project presents some noteworthy if not exceptional details that counter the late-capitalist nightmare of the adjoining Hudson Yards development. The massive commercial plan seeks to reanimate the corpse of the manufactured urban core fortress that architect John Portman epitomized with work in Detroit and Atlanta, but in particular with the Bonaventure Hotel (1976) in Los Angeles. Portman's privatized, bunker-like centerpiece projects go to startling formal lengths to convey a sense of disinterest and contempt for the public at street level. But they often include just a pinch of performative magnanimity, through evocative gestures like the eruptive emergence of the cylindrical glass elevators and atria, or the spinning lounge at the top of the Bonaventure.

The Shed has to contend with the looming, ominous proximity of Kohn Pedersen Fox's 30 Hudson Yards tower (2019), with its menacing protrusion of a shard-like observation deck, branded "The Edge." As well as perhaps the most reviled artifact of the entire development, Thomas Heatherwick's "Vessel." Some of the most engaging elements of The Shed's rolling canopy structure are its wheels, each standing almost as tall as an average person. There's an undeniable novelty in the experience of feeling slightly dwarfed by such imaginatively pragmatic, functional elements. And this impression is particularly noteworthy when those elements are in service of such a rarefied task as actually moving a building, especially in the otherwise uninspiring and dehumanizing surroundings of a quintessential quasi-public plaza. Images of The Shed's wheels populate social media and promotional imagery—such as visitors feigning effort to push the immobile wheels, or simply posing in amused adjacency next to them—and recalls footage of NASA's "crawler-transporters" slowly inching their way across a swampy headland on the Florida coast during "rollout." Laden with the skyscraper mass of a Saturn V rocket or a Space Shuttle—accompanied by a few scrawny engineers in short sleeves and black neckties, barely perceptible, strolling at a languid pace—such imagery

See: § 1, "Tiny house" (pg. 28–30).

See: MDx media, "Apollo, Saturn V, Crawler, VAB, Pad 39A - 1960 Historical Footage," YouTube, Nov. 10, 2020, [https://www.youtube.com/watch?v=7SeRUewE9To] 24:29; See also: Apollo 13 (1995, dir. Ron Howard, Universal Pictures).

… allows us to momentarily envision a future of everyday companionship with architecture, in which our routines could be characterized by tasks like taking the house out for a stroll, with the prosaic nonchalance of walking the dog. Instead, we've compromised the supposedly unsustainable spectacle of publicly funded space programs and the enormity of scale and vision that interplanetary transit demands, in exchange for a litany of privately funded projects underwritten by and named to honor the corporate executives of extractive and exploitative industries, and commissioned to punctuate and animate soulless commercial developments.

An incomplete list of building purposes:

Animal Shelter, Aquatic Center, Apartment Complex, Art Studio, Assisted Living, Bakery, Bank, Banquet Hall, Bar, Barber Shop, Barcade, Bookstore, Bowling Alley, Brewery, Cafe, Campaign Headquarters, Casino, Church, Coffee Shop, College, Community Center, Convenience Store, Convention Center, Daycare, Deli, Dentist's Office, Department Store, Diner, Dispensary, Distribution Center, DMV, Dollar Store, Dry Cleaner, Elementary School, Escape Room, Factory, Fire Department, Fitness Center, Funeral Home, Furniture Store, Gallery, Garage, Gas Station, Grocery Store, Hardware Store, Home Center, Hospital, Hotel, Laundry Mat, Law Firm, Lodge, Lounge, Mosque, Movie Theater, Museum, Office Space, Paint Store, Parking Garage, Performance Hall, Pharmacy, Photo Studio, Pizzeria, Polling Place, Power Plant, Radio Station, Recital Hall, Recreation Facility, Rehabilitation Center, Restaurant, Salon, Science Lab, Senior Center, Shoe Repair, Shopping Mall, Single Family Home, Storage Facility, Strip Club, Strip Mall, Supermarket, Taqueria, Television Studio, Temple, Theater, Trailer, Train Station, Travel Agency, Urgent Care Clinic, Veterinary Hospital, Warehouse, Yoga Studio…

§ 4 - In the built environment, **conflicts** accrue over time; the results of additions, subtractions, and divisions that inevitably come after the fact. Embedded within each conflict is a legible series of cascading events: an escalating or de-escalating skirmish between the needs and wants of how a building element should perform. Conflicts can be used to retrace the steps, to read back the transcript, and to better understand how each of these choices culminated in the present situation.

▲ ***12'-1"**

▲ Humor, along with any opportunity for irony or pun, is rare in the city surface. Unfortunately, through obstinate repetition, it seems as though the use of humor in the built environment is now regarded as the exclusive domain of "guerrilla" street artists and the likes of Banksy. Real estate markets, and capitalism's unified vision of itself more broadly, do not leave room for anything but deadened sobriety on building facades and a joyless lack of visual stimulation across the skyline.

… Any city regarded as a "financial center" or a "banking capital" is certain to eventually be drained of any formal interest or charm. This tendency directly correlates to the unimaginative veneration of architectural antiquity—the lazy idea that classical orders, along with uniformity and sobriety in building materials, gives rise to pleasing symbolic, civic, and formal relationships. Accordingly, in so many cities, the overriding principle seems to be for every permanent building element to convey a stark and serious tone. There's a bit more flexibility given to semi-permanent surfaces—say a playful visual metaphor or unexpected formal gesture found in a piece of sculpture, a bench, or maybe a bike rack. But even in large-scale public art, it's almost exclusively the monumental and self-serious that is allowed any room to operate.◆ Postmodernism was given a brief opportunity in the 1980s to disrupt this pattern, but the ambitious scale of its efforts provoked a fierce ideological retaliation from the general public, that still lingers today. It's easy to despair about the detrimental impacts of budgets and design-by-committee, but qualities like nuance and cleverness have bigger obstacles and enemies.

"WHEN ALL ELSE FAILS, TRY FOLLOWING DIRECTIONS."

▲ Routine Pleasures (1986, dir. Jean-Pierre Gorin, Channel Four Films), 00:25:23.

--- ⌖ ---

See: HRH The Prince of Wales, "Facing Up to the Future: Prince Charles on 21st Century Architecture," The Architectural Review, Dec. 20, 2014, web [https://www.architectural-review.com/essays/facing-up-to-the-future-prince-charles-on-21st-century-architecture].

◆ See: Richard Serra's entire body of work.

See: Especially, the recent struggle to preserve and fund renovations for the Portland Building (1982) by Michael Graves.

◀ We'd like to thank Aaron Fooshée for captioning the photo on the opposite page.

▲ **Slow poke**

“By its very abstraction, the grid conveyed one of the basic laws of knowledge—the separation of the perceptual screen from that of the ‘real’ world. Given all of this, it is not surprising that the grid—as an emblem of the infrastructure of vision—should become an increasingly insistent and visible feature of neo-impressionist painting [...]”

▲ Rosalind Krauss, “Grids,” October. 9 (1979): 50–64, [https://www.jstor.org/stable/778321].

For the most potent evocation of this fraught relationship, see: The Conversation (1974, dir. Francis Ford Coppola, Paramount Pictures).

… in supply lines will noticeably drop across entire cities due to the almost perfect synchronization of toilet flushes that the mass media has unwittingly enacted. It is the statistical variation of daily activities that allow for public utilities to exist and function properly, and these regulatory systems anticipate, and depend on our non-regulated choices in order to function regularly. The transformation of this anecdote into an urban legend speaks to a generalized enchantment that utilities and collective systems hold on us. The fact that we can flush away waste and (almost) never be confronted with it ever again, much less the complexities of its removal, is genuinely miraculous.

It's a shame that buildings and architectural accessories are so inhibited in their sense of propriety and boundaries. In the United States particularly, a building is almost always treated as an explicitly discrete unit—a Platonic ideal, a thing unto itself—as opposed to a messy, tangled knot of contacts and transitions of people and things moving through, over, and around each other.

This puritanical obsession with imaginary edges takes an unfortunate toll on the formal possibilities for the designed spaces surrounding us. In order to defend the infallible sanctity of arbitrary things—like property lines, air rights, and borders—we've sentenced ourselves to a landscape of redundant, repetitive monotony, and charmless predictability. It's hard not to see this extremism as directly related to the foundational violence of colonization inflicted on Indigenous peoples and populations in the United States. At every scale of life, we are constantly surrounded by artifacts and reminders, particularly in the physical manifestation of property laws. These edges are a symbolic reaffirmation; they represent an overcompensation, an insistence that the power to claim and enforce made-up territorial distinctions is derived from God, as opposed to being another mechanism for asserting force based on racism, and social, political, and economic injustice.

- - - - - -

▲ **Show-off**

▲ As a city known for exporting images, Los Angeles has developed a particular skill for generating spectacle out of the seemingly mundane activity of moving water around.

… Completed in 1965, the headquarters of the Los Angeles Department of Water and Power (LADWP) sits dramatically on Bunker Hill in Downtown, and provides a convenient example of this phenomenon. Designed by Albert C. Martin and Associates, the expansive extended floor slabs imbue the entire mass of 17 stories with a sense of gentle motion, as if the hovering structure was weightlessly transcending upward and out, like an architectural bellows. Approaching from the lower elevation of Grand Park, the building feels strangely alienated from City Hall and the Civic Center. Walking across the plaza and the fountains between Dorthy Chandler Pavilion and Mark Taper Forum, the LADWP headquarters suddenly appears to drift atop a shimmering pool of water, which conceals much of the department's parking and building systems.

The reflections of neighboring Bunker Hill skyscrapers deform and glimmer on the surface of the pools. Visiting the LADWP headquarters, you're just as likely to see department staff reporting for work as you are to find a couple, sweetly embracing or awkwardly posing in formal-wear, trailed by a photographer for their engagement announcements. Los Angeles is full of these kinds of destinations, where the work of capturing and circulating water heightens into a cinematic visual spectacle, rather than purely a logistical display. There's the Los Angeles Aqueduct Cascades at the northern edge of the San Fernando Valley, which present a grand runway to celebrate the arrival of water concluding its long journey into the city limits all the way from the Sierra Nevada Mountains. A nearby housing development took the name "The Legends at Cascades," and the surrounding community recently filed with the city for an official designation as "Rancho Cascades."

On the murkier end of the water circulation system, there's the Tillman Water Reclamation Plant in Lake Balboa, which abuts both the 405 and a wildlife reserve in the Central Valley. Here the impulse to combine apparently fantastical and unrelated thematic elements reaches a surprisingly tranquil zenith. If the odor isn't too distracting, one can meditate in the modestly spacious Japanese Garden, as over 80 million gallons of wastewater per day are being treated a few yards away. The administration building of the facility was designed by Anthony J. Lumsden; completed in 1985, it offers public viewing platforms of the treatment tanks. Perhaps the pop culture trivia fact that best testifies to the imaginative potency of the site is its role in depicting the 24th century: the Valley's wastewater treatment facility also serves as the campus of Starfleet Academy on multiple television adaptations of Star

See: § 8, "Vestigial fountain" (pg. 158-161).

See: "Portion of Sylmar To Be Renamed 'Rancho Cascades,'" Los Angeles Daily News, Oct. 4, 2018, web [https://www.dailynews.com/2018/10/04/portion-of-sylmar-to-be-renamed-rancho-cascades/].

For a discussion of the plant's relationship to other forms of architectural planting, see: Sylvia Lavin, "Reclaiming Plant Architecture," e-flux Architecture, web [https://www.e-flux.com/architecture/positions/280202/reclaiming-plant-architecture/].

... Trek (albeit with some drastic background enhancement through the use of matte paintings).

“ Note the downspouts.”

▲ Stanley Tigerman, “Stanley Tigerman Chicago Architecture,” SCI-Arc Media Archive (Southern California Institute of Architecture, Mar. 3, 1977), web [https://youtu.be/EhPuB-U34Oc?t=1656], 00:27:36.

- - - ϟ - - -

▲ **Shutter squish-to-fit**

Any opportunity to take liberties with the depiction of scale is sure to produce charming results.

Consider the signs that you see posted every 20 feet or so in most commercial parking garages, which remind you to hold on to your parking ticket for both in-store validation and for payment at the kiosk. Of course, there's the prosaic pictogram of the abstracted person, accompanied by a comparatively enormous ticket tucked cutely beneath their arm, scaled-up to the size of a piece of luggage or a giant, novelty Publishers Clearing House-esque prize check. The parking ticket seems, for the purposes of hyperbole and clarity, to have been endowed with a metaphorical heft that's either unbearable or cheerfully ludicrous. Taking liberties with sizes and scales is such an effective means to control attention and emphasis. It should really be used more often, if only for the amusement that it provides.

- - - - - -

▲ **ADA accessible sewer**

▲ The Americans with Disabilities Act of 1990 (ADA) is most often recognized for the important social justice implications associated with its enactment, and rightfully so.

Yet the ADA is commonly invoked in the context of lawsuits or other tedious anecdotes about judicial recourse that it enabled. Ironically, the least explored aspect of the law, at least discursively, could be the ADA's material dimensions: as a staggeringly efficacious intervention upon the designed surface of the country. Like few other contemporary examples, the ADA provides a powerful metaphor for the conflict between how architects and

... designers imagine spaces should look and function, and how actual people need the world to behave. Thinking about the enormous scale of its impact, one imagines that perhaps, in some overstuffed filing cabinets or dusty warehouse, there might exist an exhaustively detailed accounting of the total dimensions of material surface impacted and ultimately altered by this particular piece of legislation. These tabulations would take stock of every cubic yard of concrete and square foot of diamond plate aluminum for the millions of ramps, curb-cuts, elevator shafts, clearance width, and height alterations, all recorded in some massive spreadsheet.

The proportion of its influence boggles the mind. The most recently amended text of the ADA available on the Department of Justice's website offers a PDF totaling a humble 51 pages—not even the length of a novella. But in less than 24,000 words, the ADA has accomplished earthmoving work at a tremendously large scale. Consider the graphic language of accessibility and the litany of public domain symbols, which have now become a uniform set of contemporary glyphs for the country.✯ Such iconography is mostly seen on wayfinding and roadway signage systems, particularly those that help drivers to decrypt the complexities of the nation's parking lots and parking garages. Looking through the stencils and specification guides issued by the Federal Highway Administration (FHA) and the Department of Transportation (DOT), is like perusing a visual cipher for decoding America. It's mostly predicated around movement: icons of hikers, airplanes, snowmobiles, wheelchairs, trains, arrows up, arrows left, and arrows right. All of these abstracted Americans-on-the-move maintain tick-mark bodies and perfect circles for their disembodied, floating heads.

See: Alex MacInnis, "The Squeaky Wheelchair Gets the Grease," This American Life, ep. 415 "Crybabies," Sep. 24, 2010, web [https://www.thisamericanlife.org/415/crybabies].

Such a spreadsheet would be so physically onerous as to become an object intervention on the world in its own right, like the computer science aphorism about a digitally generated climate model so painstakingly accurate that the processing power required to run the computer program would impact the climate simulation.

✯ For a design activism and graphic icon project that questions and revises the International Symbol of Access designed in the 1960s, see: Sara Hendren, The Accessible Icon Project (2011-ongoing) [http://accessibleicon.org/].

The library symbol and the wheelchair symbol are among just a few of the common signage icons adopted to FHA and DOT standards, which actually depict a person's head attached to their body. In lieu of the comforting reassurance of bodily continuity, the vast majority of sign symbols opt for the unfortunate figure's decapitation (pedestrian, snowmobiler, equestrian, roller skater, toll collector, road worker, flagger, etc.). Perhaps this surgical sacrifice is carried out by sign-makers in the interest of cheaper printing or improved long-term material durability; most likely, it's intended to aid the semiotic legibility in the context of the highway, with its extremely narrow margins of time and velocity afforded for reading. But this coincidence speaks more to the fact that federal signage standards are populated from surprisingly diverse sources. While designers tend to imagine graphic standards as a fantasy ideal for a megalomaniacal, top-down, proscriptive approach to formal control over otherwise chaotic or incoherent systems, the Manual on Uniform Traffic Control Devices (MUTCD) issued by the DOT and FHA, seems to embody a less auteur-oriented approach. For instance, the wheelchair symbol (also known as the International Symbol of Access), was created in 1968 by Susanne Koefoed at a student design conference in Stockholm. Koefoed's original design was intended to represent only a wheelchair, which is why the circular head at the top—added later to help humanize the icon—appears so precariously placed, teetering from the vertical projection that was originally the back of the chair. The abstracted profile of a library patron holding the fanned pages of a book on the general information roadway sign for libraries was designed in 1978 by Ralph E. DeVore for the Western Maryland Regional Library, then endorsed by the American Library Association, and accepted by the FHA for inclusion in the MUTCD national sign standards in 1985.

▲ Work-arounds

▲ Working in architectural design software today is to find oneself dipping into a pungent bouillabaisse of vaguely intimidating mathematical jargon and operations increasingly supported by the insights of artificial intelligence.

But thanks to the thoughtful efforts of interaction designers and user experience designers, one's productive capacities are rarely stifled by a lack of deep technical understanding of these terms. You can just soak in the various affordances and outputs, and familiarity will eventually start to permeate. For instance, the method for representing curves in computer

... graphics, particularly in drawing and drafting software, is largely credited to Pierre Bézier, who made use of Bernstein polynomials in a method very similar to Paul de Casteljau. Both men were working on ways to apply emerging digital tools in the 1950s and 1960s to more precisely describe the bulging fenders and swooping tails of the automotive body—Bézier for Renault and de Casteljau for Citroën. Curves, of course, were a major preoccupation for engineers and developers in the early days of computer design software. And while we aren't necessarily called upon to scrupulously consider the finer points and mathematical basis of the curve today, it is still disquieting, if not downright humbling, to reflect on the mountain of scratched out equations and chalkboard calculations on which our buildings are predicated.

--- ---

§ 5 - Coverings always come last, receiving the least intention or consideration, as a hurried attempt to obscure, redact, and remove elements—to redirect attention. Whether through wrapping, draping, enveloping, filling, camouflaging, pasting, painting, or masking, it is impossible to remove all traces of what is covered.

▲ **Transparent drywall**

▲ Perhaps the most lasting realization that lingers with you—following some otherwise tedious and mercifully brief period of home renovation, demolition, and construction—is the extent to which interior finishes are simply a method for covering up the otherwise impressive and fascinating interrelationships of building systems and structural methods.

Any opportunity to expose the underlying spacing and regularity of 2×4 studs reveals the satisfying clarity and delightful simplicity of platform framing. Interspersed among the studs, there's the triumphant sense of urgency and momentum in parallel columns of copper pipes, or the elegant curving elbows

… of brushed aluminum rigid conduit, or the creepy tentacular coiling of helical flex conduit. These elements produce a visible diagram for the otherwise inscrutable complexities embodied in the apparently mystical relationships between light bulbs and light switches, thermostats and radiators, faucets and drains, and all of the other touch-points providing control and comfort in domestic space. But so much labor, material, and time-intensive precision scrutiny is expended on hiding all of these interesting bits with monotonous, standardized uniformity. Of course, the half-timber construction of the Tudor style had the common sense to visibly expose and celebrate the wonders of load-bearing elements on the exterior, which makes the "Mock" Tudors occasionally found in the suburbs or housing developments all the more tacky. In the domestic interior, your field of vision is mostly occupied by an expanse of painted plaster or drywall, with the accent of baseboards or trim as the few instances of visual interruption. ✕ The unfinished basement, or perhaps the garage, is the rare space of exception, in which pragmatic and functional concerns take precedence, and the delightful informality of exposed joists, studs, pipes, and wiring have a moment to shine. It's no wonder that the garage and basement exude such potent and visceral associations in contemporary American culture as a place of either tremendous productive capacity—like the garage in Silicon Valley's founding mythos—or as a place of tremendous discomfort, as with the basement in almost any horror film.

The use of the term "unfinished" for such spaces speaks to a sense of unfulfilled potential: any interior space can be wonderful, given sufficient finishings. And finishing is largely just covering and concealing. Perhaps to "finish" a garage or a basement is to truly temper the environment—to remove the edgy, uncomfortable sense of indeterminacy that exposed studs reveal—and impose a fixed, settled permanence. Hiding the rough edges with more fine-grained finishes and obscuring the nakedness of component parts, like plumbing and wiring, provides a comfortable assurance that the home is "fixed" and "finished," suitable for living.

- - □□□ - -

✕ For numerous playful subversions and amplifications of this otherwise banal observation, see: The McCormick Tribune Campus Center (2003, OMA) on the campus of the Illinois Institute of Technology.

See, for example: Shelly and Leo Johnson's house, in a perpetual state of indeterminacy, with exposed stud walls and plastic sheeting, in Twin Peaks (1990-1991, 2017, creators Mark Frost and David Lynch).

▲ **Funeral pall**

▲ The word tarp is an abbreviation of tarpaulin, which is a compound of tar and pall—a piece of pall covered with tar to make it water-resistant.

Around the turn of the last century, tarpaulin was mostly associated with sailors, who would tar their own pall in order to have enough reliably water-resistant canvas available to protect equipment and cargo on the deck.

... In the era of stacked, standardized shipping containers, and their attendant Ultra Large Container Ships, today tarp is less evocative of ocean-going vessels, and is an evidentiary artifact associated with the impacts of catastrophic weather events linked to climate change and housing insecurity. Following a single, unprecedented storm—or perhaps an entire unprecedented season of storms—news coverage will invariably portray a sea of bright-blue enveloped roofs on single-family homes across the coastal American South. And any depiction of "homeless encampments" will invariably include the ubiquitous woven blue polyethylene surface of tarp shelters.

But tarpaulin also plays an iconic role as a symbolic object in the second act of Sergei Eisenstein's cinematically formative Battleship Potemkin (1925). Revolting over some bad borscht, a group of sailors are corralled on the foredeck in order to be dispatched by an impromptu firing squad. The commander gives an order and a contingent of officers marches a haphazard bundle of canvas over to the condemned men. The lumpen roll of cloth resembles a crumpled corpse until unfurled and dramatically strewn across the doomed sailors in two rapid sequences of opposing movement across the frame. After the sailor's revolt begins, and the men escape execution, they toss off the shroud and the camera lingers on its empty mass for a few additional seconds, as a gentle breeze provides the cloth with a spectral, momentary ambulation.

⊘ See: § 5, "Modesty veil" (pg. 132-134).

We mostly hear the term "pall" used in a related sense, referring to a fragment of cloth used to cover coffins or tombs, but it might also be used to underscore the ominous qualities of clouds of fog or smoke, evoking once again the repercussions of routine natural disasters, particularly catastrophic forest fires. In more everyday circumstances, the tarp has entered into the disreputable company of certain prosaic objects comprising the lexicon of universal signifiers of malfunction. Any object wrapped in a tarp—or its functional relative, the humble black trash bag—has been designated as "out of order" and unworthy of use,⊘ whether it be a self-service gas station pump, a toilet, or perhaps a group of revolutionarily inclined, borscht-averse sailors.

- - - - - -

▲ **Wardrobe malfunction**

▲ Although they surround us constantly, the prosaic building components that provide a comfortable, stable, and dry interior climate often go unsung, sadly. This modest ensemble is composed

… of siding, cladding, shingles, housewrap, insulation, and framing.

There's a callous obliviousness in the weight of expectation we bestow upon these diligent coverings, envelopes, and enclosures. In selflessly carrying out their functions, we're able to sleep more soundly, work more efficiently, and shop more voraciously. The fact that we only take a moment to regard them in their embarrassing instances of failure exposes the one-sidedness of this relationship.

As if to call attention to our self-absorbed sense of disappointment in the betrayal inflicted by a leaky roof or a crumbling wall, there is the emphatic visibility of the glowing, bright blue all-purpose poly tarp. Among the most affordable means of recourse in addressing the deficiencies of building materials, your local hardware store offers small tarp sheets suitable to cover a hole in the roof for ten dollars, or a vast, folded mass that could cover the entire house for $150. In fact, across the broad spectrum of dimensions on offer, it's a product that is surprisingly consistent in its pricing. Blue tarp almost always retails for five cents per square foot. That ubiquitous radiant color application designates it as "light duty" within the confounding palette of various tarp thicknesses: starting with the thinner light-duty blue, then ascending to yellow/orange, green, silver, and finally, heavy-duty brown. The fact that tarp manufacturers are inconsistent in their adherence to this coding system makes its usefulness all the more questionable.

But one doesn't need a color-coded system to understand this is a textile that bears a dizzying variety of duties. It is a material surface that, like so few others, calls out to the immediacy of a need being met; a prosaic object taking on a responsibility. As with the infamous term "wardrobe malfunction," a coinage employed in order to convey a dull, bureaucratic tone in discussions surrounding the visibility of "intimate" body parts, the poly tarp itself, in its employment as a covering, exposes cultural assumptions about performance, propriety, and duration in the structures around us.

The ambition of so many building materials aspires to the indefinite promise of a "lifetime." The question of who's lifetime is never explicated. The poly tarp is found at points of contact between functionality and failure, between intimacy and exposure. And as such, it exposes the discomforting limits of material performance, like a bright blue Sharpie® highlighter

See: § 5, "Funeral pall" (pg. 118-119).

This apocryphal color-coding system—which purportedly indicates, or rather hints at, the density of a given tarp—is reminiscent of the color coding used for those ubiquitous, flat plastic bread clips notched onto the spun length of bags containing bagels, English muffins, or loaves of bread at the grocery store. If the bag is the humble domicile of the baked good, then these plastic tags are a latch on the door. It's a disarmingly simple means for sinching the bag shut, and a much more satisfying mechanism than their nemesis, the twist tie, which is really nothing more than a glorified length of thin gauge wire. These flat plastic tags possess a particularly fussy quality in their strangely specific angles and articulated curves. Interrogating their formal language is like evaluating a carton of milk or a …

… emphatically scrawled across the building surface, invasively calling attention back to the fallibility of the environments where we heedlessly find temporary shelter.

… shopping cart; these artifacts are so embedded in the everyday routines of consumer life as to be almost completely transparent. But there's a sense of legibility and coherency of purpose in the bread clip, which is reassuring in a space where evaluation is so critical. The grocery store is uniquely a place in which we reckon with two extremely distinct time frames. On one end, there's the immediacy of the fresh, typically within days or a week of purchase for breads, fruits, vegetables, meats, and dairy. And on the other hand, there's the expansive timelessness of boxed and canned goods, on which we only check the "best by" stamps in the most dire of circumstances. While the "best by" tag is urgent and decisive in its precision and conviction, the poly tarp and the humble little bread clip are more subtle and suggestive in the message they're intended to convey—an extra bonus layer of meaning embedded in the color scheme: cyan for items baked on Monday, then Tuesday's green, crimson for Thursday, Friday with white, and yellow for Saturday (evidently, Wednesday and Sunday are days off for the bakers). A fluency in this code could provide a consumer with an expedient tool for evaluating the freshness of items in the bakery department, but more realistically, it's part of the coded language of logistics, simply a quick means for the stockers to rotate items on and off the shelf.

▲ **Paint Bucket Tool tolerance**

▲ Occasionally the overly hasty efforts of a painting crew, equipped with a pressure paint sprayer and an insufficient supply of masking tape, will result in an entire apartment façade covered in a uniform coat of beige, including not only the stucco exterior wall, but also the street numbers, “For Rent” signs, lamps, and lightbulbs.

Though the building owner may not regard this as a desirable outcome, it’s an admirably scrupulous application of the “Paint Bucket tool” logic of hiding communications equipment, lighting systems, and electrical devices. Each additional piece of equipment that receives this kind of

See: § 1, “Clever disguise” (pg. 34-35).
See: § 1, “MY COMPANY NAME THERE” (pg. 32-33); See also: “Golden Arches: Alternate versions,” Wikipedia, n.d. [https://en.wikipedia.org/wiki/Golden_Arches#Alternate_versions]

... camouflage appliqué serves as a probe for the limits of propriety and visual acceptability in the everyday domestic landscape. Like the infamously comprehensive community development regulations of various municipalities that have compelled McDonald’s to alter its branded color scheme in order to satisfy their particularly exhaustive expectations of visual satisfaction in the built environment.

> “Tired of filling in a closed area with the Paint Bucket tool, and it leaving a small thin outline around the area you wanted to fill in! ME TOO! That’s why I’m here asking around, lol. 😃 ... I’m being silly, but in all seriousness, I have had this problem for a few years now and have never actually found an answer to this problem. 🤔 ... I know Photoshops Bucket Tool should be capable of this, because on my crappy 1st gen. iPad mini I have a program called ArtStudio. It’s a travel sized art program that has about 1/4th the capability of Photoshop, and it... it has masted this ‘One click with the Bucket tool, and an area is filled!’ problem!!! In ArtStudio the ‘Normal Mode’ setting on the Paint Bucket creates the same effect as the Photoshop Paint Bucket. If the ‘Smart Mode’ setting is selected in the Paint Bucket settings, it creates a solid color fill... IN ONE CLICK! 😀 I love Photoshop, its one of my favorite art programs, but I feel like if this little travel sized IOS art program can do this, then Photoshop should be more then capable of this too. Please if you know how to fix this ‘Filling in the area WITH ONLY the Bucket Tool, IN ONE CLICK’ problem please... PLEASE share your wisdom and let me know. This is my biggest and only complaint with Photoshop and fixing this/know this would make my day! 😎”

▲ AmberGold, “Is there a way to make the Paint Bucket Tool actually fill a selection witout [sic] leaving an outline?,” Adobe Support Community, Jul. 09, 2018, web, [https://community.adobe.com/t5/photoshop/is-there-a-way-to-make-the-paint-bucket-tool-actually-fill-a-selection-witout-leaving-an-outline/td-p/9920413?page=1].

- - - 💻 - - -

▲ **Aspirational vinyl**

▲ The rise of industrialization and its massive, undecipherable systems of material production, circulation, and distribution, presents us with a provocative dual outcome for conceptualizing and carrying out contemporary architecture and building practices.

… The first outcome regards the emergent constellation of almost uniform big-box home improvement stores across the United States. And the second outcome reveals the ability for industry to offer hyper-specialized building products, like engineered components and systems. The former is seen as more amateur oriented, accessible, everyday, mundane, and ubiquitous. The latter is regarded as worthy of inclusion in the practice of architecture, as more advanced and exclusive. But these two realms are not so far apart. Efforts to enforce the boundaries of the field—to emphatically dictate what is architecture and what is not, to resolutely define who has relevant design knowledge and who does not—have been reliably stable since at least the rise of accreditation and professional licensing. But around the edges of practice, there are increasing examples that expose the flimsiness of these distinctions. The professional and the prosaic share more and more of the same territory: first on the construction site, then in the office, and eventually in the studio and classroom.

> “ This generally intellectual character of the panoramic vision is further attested by the following phenomenon, which Hugh and Michelet had moreover made into the mainspring of their bird's-eye views: to perceive Paris from above is infallibly to imagine a history; from the top of the Tower, the mind finds itself dreaming of the mutation of the landscape which it has before its eyes; through the astonishment of space, it plunges into the mystery of time, lets itself be affected by a kind of spontaneous anamnesis: it is duration itself which becomes panoramic.”
>
> ▲ Roland Barthes, “The Eiffel Tower,” The Eiffel Tower and Other Mythologies (Berkeley, CA: University of California Press, 1979), 11.

- - - - - -

▲ **Disposable armor**

▲ Among so many other fraught topics, the discussion around monuments and memorialization in the United States has been mind-numbingly constrained.⁕

Inherent in so much of the publicly engaged discourse concerning who gets memorialized and where, is the lack of apparent interest in the role of the public. This reflects a broader unwillingness to seriously reckon with issues of removal, redaction, and defacement. More than anything else, this points to an embarrassing inferiority complex: the panicked obsession with accumulating cultural signifiers and never relinquishing anything that once held civic meaning. All memorials and monuments are subjective; the problem is rooted in how we view objectivity in public space. Ultimately, a statue embodies a conversation about memory, significance, and meaning,

… and the state's unwillingness, or at best hesitancy, to present such topics as fluid shouldn't be surprising.

✲ There are significant contemporary conversations, scholarship, and art practices currently working to open up these discussions and address issues presented by monuments and historical markers. For a recent conversation at the intersection of these topics see: La Vaughn Belle, Nicholas Galanin, Dell Upton, Tsione Wolde-Michael, and Tiffany Cain, "As the Statues Fall: A Conversation about Monuments and the Power of Memory," *Vimeo*, Wenner-Gren Foundation, Jul. 23, 2020 [https://vimeo.com/439042290];

See also: The exhibitions and art work of Karyn Olivier, including *The Battle Is Joined*, 2017, Public Art Commission Monument Lab, Mural Arts, Vernon Park, Philadelphia; and *Moving the Obelisk*, 2019-20, American Academy in Rome and ICA Philadelphia.

▲ **Interpretive ambiguity**

In Rome, it's satisfying to be presented with a sense of legibility inherent in the effort and upkeep of the signage, markers, and displays.

The extent to which anyone has bothered (or received sufficient funding) to offer a reasonably coherent translation—much less even labeled, dated, and described a site or artifact at all with a view to the public's accessibility—communicates another chapter of the story. Then there's the signage at Ostia Antica, much of which has been bleached uniformly white due to the southern exposure of the site's layout and the sunny Mediterranean climate. The lettering of the signs is ever-so-slightly embossed; reading the white-on-white text is inadvisable, but nevertheless possible. Given an unreasonable investment of time and effort, the interpretive messaging can be decrypted. It's nice to imagine that such optical labor provides us with a meaningful or poetic metaphor for the legibility of history itself.

"You wouldn't expect dirty yellow crooked bricks to look pretty, but they did, especially where you could see places in the wall where there had been old windows or old doorways that had been stuffed with other bricks and stones and pieces of old buildings. That was what a certain memory that you had forgotten felt like—you knew that a window had been there but it wasn't now, just an old brick wall, so you couldn't see through it."
▸ Nicholson Baker, The Everlasting Story of Nory (New York: Vintage Books, 1999), 29.

Many interpretive signs and historical displays found along roadways in the United States so often seem to be sneakily skirting complicated topics and coyly avoiding counter-narratives. In many cases, we're left with the distinct sense of a "yada yada yada" mentality applied to vast swaths of contested details. Think of some lonely spot near a highway denoted with the amusingly recursive "Historical Marker →" sign, a marker to indicate a marker. Such roadside pull-offs always look like vestigial spaces hanging precariously off the highway, meekly offering three or four parking spots to accompany the main attraction: a solemn cast bronze plaque nestled in an inclined concrete plinth and garnished with a few steel barriers. For those who can be bothered to stop and read—almost always just a pretense to exit the car for a moment and stretch one's road-weary muscles—the interpretive text often offers a disturbingly triumphant, authoritative, and hostile narrative: an act of "exploring" and "settling" carried out by a colonizer or enslaver, with perhaps only an aside about the Indigenous population.

▲ **Riverbend access door**

▲ Until the early 1990s, the capacity of Computer-Generated Imagery (CGI) to produce a depiction of "live action" convincing enough to appear "real" was ludicrously out of reach.

... Some scattered examples of short CGI sequences in films from the 1960s through the 1980s are largely constrained to rudimentary 2-D animation or vector wireframe models. But the impressive ambition to integrate digital renderings with filmed imagery, though still far from convincing, is characterized in the 1990s by such examples as Terminator 2: Judgment Day (1991, dir. James Cameron), Jurassic Park (1993, dir. Steven Spielberg), Apollo 13 (1995, dir. Ron Howard), and Twister (1996, dir. Jan de Bont). The wave of advancements in computer hardware and rendering algorithms gave way to larger budget CGI that could ambitiously attempt to pass for "real life." Then at the turn of the century, blockbuster cinema entered a sort of uncanny valley in representation. Despite the embarrassing giveaways of low-quality texture maps, erratic movements, and incomprehensible lighting, there is a reassuring sense of security in watching films in which the line between physical spaces and digital fabrications is plainly recognizable, as in Star Wars: Episode I – The Phantom Menace (1999, dir. George Lucas), The Matrix Reloaded (2003, dirs. Lana Wachowski and Lilly Wachowski), I Am Legend (2007, dir. Francis Lawrence), and especially The Mummy Returns (2001, dir. Stephen Sommers). In each of these films, there are charming instances of inchoate digital effects, usually captured in the unrealistic flutter of a computer-inserted cape or trench coat, or the unconvincingly stiff, thick, rubbery folds in some fantastical creature's skin, or the utter forfeiture of attempting to model hair (conveniently enough, most examples from the era feature creatures and characters that are bald or otherwise hairless). The viewer doesn't have to look closely to catch these moments; they practically jump off the screen in their artificiality. Ironically, these digitally augmented scenes stand out because they specifically disrupt one's ability to suspend disbelief, to be enraptured and entranced by the magic of filmmaking.

See: § 2, "Uncanny valley" (pg. 70-71).

As digital representations become the predominant imagery shaping our routine experiences and understanding of the environments around us, our capacity to recognize, read, influence, edit, reject, and undermine the objectivity and apparent immutability of those depictions is increasingly urgent. The comfort of clearly identifying CGI—of being able to tell the difference between what is "real" and what is "live action"—sits in stark contrast to the discomfort in the contemporary era of fake news and deepfakes, and the creeping dread pointing to an inevitable future in which reality increasingly appears indistinguishable from CGI.

See: Oscar Ruiz, "Houses, Mexico," National Geographic, May 8, 2013, web [https://www.nationalgeographic.com/photography/photo-of-the-day/2013/5/housing-development-mexico/].

“ In the course of Time, these Extensive maps were found somehow wanting, and so the College of Cartographers evolved a Map of the Empire that was of the same Scale as the Empire and that coincided with it point for point.”

▲ Jorge Luis Borges, “Of Exactitude in Science,” A Universal History of Infamy, trans. Norman Thomas di Giovanni (New York: E.P. Dutton & Co., Inc., 1970), 141.

▲ **Modesty veil**

◂ Signs in the urban environment often seem to be speaking to us—shouting, whispering, seducing, mumbling, or murmuring as simultaneous overheard conversations visualized through the streetscape.

In this sense, driving down Pico Boulevard or the Sunset Strip in Los Angeles is not so different from scrolling through social media, a sequence strung together by disparate voices, topics, and tones. One moment a cute cat, the next moment a horrifyingly violent police confrontation. One moment a frenetically edited cake recipe, the next moment an earnest reflection on an internalized experience of assault. In the cityscape, every building provides its own discrete invocation to some need, service, or desire, and the journey itself, the "route," is the only thing stringing them together in a sequence. Now that social media increasingly dominates and dictates our experience of public discourse and interpersonal relationships, it's tempting to imagine that our capacity to absorb increasingly radical formal and functional adjacencies in the landscapes around us could change dramatically. Visiting our parents in the suburbs recently, we drove past the former location of their town's Bank of America branch, which had been transformed into a recreational marijuana dispensary. As a bank, the fact that this building shared a block with a cosmetology school, a candy store, and a funeral home seemed unremarkable. But the addition of the dispensary suddenly calls this entire constellation of meanings into question.

“ A convenience store is not merely a place where customers come to buy practical necessities, it has to be somewhere they can enjoy and take pleasure in discovering things they like. [...] I could hear the store's voice telling me what it wanted, how it wanted to be. I understood it perfectly. [...] I couldn't stop hearing the store telling me the way it wanted to be, what it

... needed. It was all flowing into me. It wasn't me speaking. It was the store. I was just channeling its revelations from on high."

▲ Sayaka Murata, Convenience Store Woman, trans. by Ginny Tapley Takemori (New York: Grove Press, 2016), 159-160.

▲ **Ready-to-assemble forest**

The tradition of picturesque landscape painting—like more recent practices of internet surfing and web design—relies on the imposition of a frame.

In an essay on landscape painting, historian Monique Mosser discusses the "symbolic reduction" of perspective and the "physical removal of the subject" as a means to "appropriate a fragment of the world." Later in the article, she offers a quotation from Roland Recht to elaborate on the connection between one's search for spatial continuum in the landscape, and early devices of optical illusion:

> "... the spectator chooses an object of contemplation and then creates a frame for it: i.e. a delimitation of the visual field used, first, to exclude everything overly distant from the chosen object from within its borders; and, second, to retain around the chosen object those components necessary for sustaining its inscription in the spatial continuum."

Without the background to distinguish the foreground, everything just falls away. Whether the foreground or the background takes our central focus seems to be a reliable source of contention for designers. The apparent primacy of one approach or another precludes any easy answer. This isn't a new discussion, but perhaps we shouldn't feel so encumbered by it. In writing about considerations for the design of period rooms in 1917, Virginia Robie notes that: "Backgrounds in the broadest sense were seldom considered, for proportion, balance and scale were foreign terms to most householders and to many decorators." Later in the article, she suggests that: "Of late the architect has again come into his [sic] own, and the golden age of architectural backgrounds has been restored."

\- - - ❁ - - -

Monique Mosser, "The Roving Eye: Panoramic Décors and Landscape Theory," French Scenic Wallpaper 1795–1865, ed. Odile Nouvel-Kammerer (Paris: Flammarion, 2001), 195 and 207.

Virginia Robie, "Backgrounds," The Art World, Vol. 2 No. 5 (1917), 477 and 478-9, accessed April 25, 2016, [https://www.jstor.org/stable/25588062].

For an earlier and expanded version of this text, see our essay "On Background," Offramp, no. 11, Los Angeles: SCI-Arc Press, web [https://offramp.sciarc.edu/issues].

▲ **Air conditioning conditioner**

▲ In 2004, Polaroid issued a statement warning consumers that, contrary to popular belief, they should not "shake it like a Polaroid picture" when waiting for their images to self-develop.

... Of course, the pop song refrain from the year prior was much catchier than the more practical lyrics to “lay it on a flat surface like a Polaroid picture.” But, in fact, vigorously shaking the photograph can actually damage the image while it develops. It seems as though this practice of shaking self-developing film in an attempt to help the chemical development process along is actually a hold-over from a time in which the film didn’t have a clear plastic window protecting the image, as was implemented in later Polaroid film manufacturing. Historically, waving the photograph in order to expose the print surface to more air could actually help it to dry faster. In doing so, Polaroid film entered that rarified field of consumer products with a highly specific, tangibly satisfying ritual attached, like the impulse to swing a packet of sugar back and forth across a pinched thumb and finger, to tap a pack of cigarettes in the palm, or to “burp” the lid of a Tupperware® container. In the case of Polaroid film, the technology advanced beyond the user’s ritualistic associations, resulting in a disjunction between how it works and how it is perceived to work. Similar to a catchy lyric that gets stuck in your head, once a certain understanding gets concretized in the collective conscious, it’s difficult to remove.

A window awning mounted above an air conditioning unit possesses a similar mentality as a conceptual hold-over: an almost spiritual association, which posits that efforts should be made to shade and cool the device producing coolness—a reasonable assumption. This inadvertently produces a highly didactic display on the genealogy of cooling technologies, a sort of family tree diagram. It’s reminiscent of “The Road to Homo Sapiens,” the iconic illustration with a cavorting, care-free Pliopithecus on the far left, and a humorless, haunted-looking “Modern Man” on the far right, populated by a parade of striding primates representing 25 million years of human evolution in between them. The obsolete falls in line behind its replacement. In the case of the miniature awning, it remains in service of its usurper—the window air conditioner.

One imagines the same scene a few years in the future: the same awning providing shelter from the sun for the same air-conditioning unit, puttering away after years of service and now enlisted to keep cool a newer, more powerful and effective piece of technology that has replaced it.

“ It’s a new kind of physical information architecture: windowless boxes, often with distinct design features, such as an appliqué of surface graphics, or a functional

“Polaroid warns buyers not to ‘shake it,’” CNN, Feb. 18, 2004, web [http://www.cnn.com/2004/TECH/ptech/02/17/polaroid.warns.reut/index.html].

See: Rudolph Zallinger, “The Road to Homo Sapiens,” (also titled “The March of Progress”), Life Nature Library: Early Man (New York: Time-Life, 1965), 41-45.

... brutalism, surrounded by cooling systems. A building that is a machine tended by a small staff of technicians and security guards."

▲ "Networked Nation: The Landscape of the Internet in America," (Culver City: The Center for Land Use Interpretation, Nov. 3, 2013).

--- ---

§ 6 - Edges exist as wide regions or thin lines, they can be inhabitable or implied, physical or conceptual, spoken or unspoken. Despite their varied presence, edges always mediate between two things and it is in this area of mediation where frictions and tangible discomforts arise, especially in moments of ambiguity.

▲ **Machine vision eye test**

> “The vOICe can never successfully translate the visual experience of looking at his wife’s face or watching the sun set over the snow-covered mountains outside Banff. But, he added, ‘vinyl siding makes a very nice sound, actually, like music almost. So there’s a beauty in that.’”

▲ Nicola Twilley, “Seeing with Your Tongue,” The New Yorker, May 15, 2017.

There's an ever-increasing tediousness to the onslaught of anecdotes about the quirks of digital databases used to train machine learning algorithms.

It's surprising how rapidly headlines that once seemed so novel (typically something along the lines of "A Programmer Trained This AI To Write Hundreds of Quentin Tarantino Movie Scripts") have become entirely banal. But beyond the emerging trope of "We trained a bot to do x using y," the question of how digital databases are populated, and what information and imagery populates them, feels more insistent and invasive each day. The anxiety isn't so much about stumbling across imagery of yourself or data regarding your personal life within the AI training databases of some defunct startup. After all, the defining metric of these databases is their indefatigable exhaustiveness. Even if you were motivated to make certain that images of yourself, your family, and friends shared on social media were not being used to train facial recognition software for military and police forces across the world, the data is proprietary, and the quantity of information required to review would require multiple human lifetimes. Instead, this quietly malignant relationship—between our personal lives and the platforms exploiting our interactions, transactions, and everyday experiences for marketable insights—generates a more persistent sense of anxiety that lingers in the background, only rarely coming to the surface. As more and more of our lives are framed and dictated by online platforms, such isolated anecdotes today are certain to become more commonplace in the future. These examples provide a bit more specificity to the abstract threat suggested whenever somebody invokes the trope about social media and apps: "if it's free, then you're the product."

But beyond the sense of bodily, personal discomfort elicited from long-forgotten uploads of digital photos from birthday parties, reunions, housewarmings, and baby showers being used to train facial recognition algorithms, the apparent banality and harmlessness of Google Street View is even more sinister. The totalizing ambition to map, photograph, scan, and digitally model every square inch of the world's surface is as clear a statement as one could imagine for capturing Google's self-image as an institution that looks solely to determine the invasiveness of technology in our collective lives. These ambitions achieve a striking material output as an ersatz sculpture park near their headquarters in Mountain View, California, also known as the Googleplex,

Rachel Moss, "This Is What It's Like to Be Targeted by Baby Ads After Miscarriage or IVF Struggles," HuffPost UK, Sep. 9, 2019, web, accessed Dec. 27, 2020, web [https://www.huffingtonpost.co.uk/entry/women-affected-by-miscarriage-and-infertility-are-being-targeted-with-baby-ads-on-facebook_uk_5d7f7c42e4b00d69059bd88a].

Kashmir Hill and Aaron Krolik, "How Photos of Your Kids Are Powering Surveillance Technology: Millions of Flickr images were sucked into a database called MegaFace. Now some of those faces may have the ability to sue," The New York Times, Oct. 11, 2019, web, accessed Oct. 27, 2019, web [https://www.nytimes.com/interactive/2019/10/11/technology/flickr-facial-recognition.html].

... where a buffet of exterior building treatments and surfaces are arranged in a Stonehenge-like perimeter around a parking lot in a lesser-visited corner of the sprawling Bay Area campus. These structures, each about eight feet wide and about four feet tall, are decontextualized samples of the conventional American neighborhood, some featuring white vinyl siding, or simple brickwork, or other combinations of cladding and masonry, and occasionally punctuated with fussy electrical boxes, spigots, or exhaust vent hoods. Even the surface of the parking lot itself offers a "variety pack" of roadways and pavings, including different styles and arrangements of brick, asphalt, and concrete.

This impromptu monument to the humble, uncelebrated exterior would otherwise be delightful, if not for the circumstances. For a moment, it feels like a preemptive veneration of things usually reserved for the category of nostalgia and kitsch. It's the display you might expect to find in some roadside "museums" along Historic Route 66, which seek to idolize the remembered halcyon characteristics of post-war, small-town Americana by faithfully recreating or preserving candy stores, gas stations, and diners of the era. Such tourist attractions seem to be exclusively visited by RV-wielding retirees and the occasional busload of German tourists. This doe-eyed, rose-tinted sentimentality towards the manufactured American landscape feels particularly at odds in Silicon Valley, with its pervasive reputation for upholding an unwavering faith and focus on the future.

Unfortunately, this exhibition in an anonymous parking lot of the Googleplex is driven by preservation of a different sort: these building samples calibrate and test the photographic and machine vision capabilities of the arrayed sensors outfitting their fleet of Street View Cars. It is not a sculpture park, but rather, a proving ground. The usual motivations for amassing and exhibiting a collection—a sense of appreciation and the desire to share that feeling with other people—is absent. Google's proving ground betrays an indifference to context and adjacency; the edges of the material surfaces are blunt and the transitions are unrefined. Standing among these clumsy tributes to the Age of Algorithms is like reading the 10-year projected release schedule that movie studios occasionally announce, with all of the cinematic romance and emotional subtlety stripped away to reveal the blunt, commercial pragmatism of artwork that could very well become meaningful, inspiring, heart-wrenching statements of the human condition, here listed in chronological bullet point

… as “Untitled Live-Action 2027” and “Untitled Animation 2028.”

Of course, we’ve become inured to the insistent pleas, constantly issued from every technology company imaginable, that they’re motivated only by a heroic, uncompromising impulse to usher society into an impending techno-utopia (if we would all simply adopt their particular product suite). Google’s interest is in developing software and hardware that can reconcile the material realities in which we find ourselves living, to make sense of it for the purposes of machine applications, not necessarily for human applications. And since machine vision protocols and neural net algorithms are poorly suited to consider how issues such as policing, activism, gentrification, housing insecurity, and access to transit and government services are related to the material realities of the built environment, the teams of engineers, supervisors, and managers who oversee this work have decided to exonerate themselves from considering it as well.

> “ Thus, perspective, which until now served as a model of visual automation, becomes the drawback that needs to be overcome. Perspective, this first step towards the rationalization of sight (Ivins) has eventually become a limit to its total rationalization—the development of computer vision.”

▲ Lev Manovich, “Automation of Sight: From Photography to Computer Vision,” (1997), 13. [http://manovich.net/index.php/projects/automation-of-sight-from-photography-to-computer-vision]

▲ **Decorative shed**

“ Sometimes I lie in bed at three or four in the morning and I imagine myself flying miles above the earth, very cold, and one of those black secret spy planes is up there with the huge round engines with the spinning blades in it, the blades that look like the underside of mushrooms? The black plane's going very fast in the opposite direction and we intersect, and I fly right through one of those jet engines, and I exit as this long fog of blood. I'm miles long, and, because it's so cold, I'm crystalline. [...] And then I recondense in bed, sshhp, as my short warm self.”

▲ Nicholson Baker, Vox (New York: Vintage Contemporaries, 1993), 95-96.

By 1920, enough capital investment circulated through Hollywood productions for the industry to start leaving a noticeable, if not impermanent, material impression on the region's constructed landscape.

The bulging, overly enstasis-ized columns and squatting row of enormous caryatid elephants constructed across multiple blocks of the current day Los Feliz neighborhood for D.W. Griffith's <u>Intolerance</u> (1916) were simply left standing in place for nearly four years after the production was complete, towering over the area as a monument to cinematic ambition and excess (and to be reanimated by mall developers in November 2001 as a centerpiece of the unimaginatively titled Hollywood & Highland shopping center). Through the 1920s, the novel structural expertise of the aerospace industry also contributed to a fortuitously skilled labor market that—combined with the influence of set-building expertise—would prove a decisive combination for the regional emergence of Streamline Moderne and Googie architecture. The starbursts, fins, and boomerangs characteristic of these early responses to car culture embody the ambition of emerging formal expression in the cityscape that would shape Los Angeles's architecture in the decades that followed.✹ But the unique and precise application of expert trades to sculpt plaster, stucco, wood, and wire into fantastical assemblages really takes its most memorable shape in what would eventually earn the category recognition as programmatic architecture. Most of these buildings represented either food products or mechanical engineering icons, such as trains, airplanes, boats, zeppelins, and even an oil can. While the aerospace industry in Los Angeles receded from prominence, it's telling that the more memorable examples, and those more likely to be maintained and still popular today, are mostly emblems of food rather than transit:

- ❏ <u>The Brown Derby</u> (1926, bowler hat-as-restaurant)
- ❏ <u>The Cream Can</u> (1928, milk can-as-dairy retailer)
- ❏ <u>The Tamale</u> (1928, tamale-as-tamale stand, now a beauty salon)
- ❏ <u>The Hollywood Flower Pot</u> (1930, flower pot and flower-as-flower shop)
- ❏ <u>The Chili Bowl</u> (1931, chili bowl-as-restaurant)
- ❏ <u>Coca-Cola Bottling Building</u> (1939, ocean liner-as-bottling factory)
- ❏ <u>Idle Hour</u> (1941, beer keg-as-taproom)
- ❏ <u>Tail o' the Pup</u> (1946, hot dog-as-hot dog stand)
- ❏ <u>Big Donut Drive-In</u> (1953, donut-as-donut shop sign, now Randy's Donuts)

✹ See: The prolific architectural design work of Paul R. Williams, including The Gertrude and Harry Kaye Building (1948), The Ambassador Hotel (Renovation 1949, Demolished 2006), The Paul R. Williams Residence (1952), and The Theme Building at Los Angeles International Airport (1961) with William Pereira, Charles Luckman, Gin D. Wong, and Welton Becket, among others.

▲ **Facial storage**

With its tidy grid lines, satisfying arrangements of concrete chocks, swooping curb cuts, and grassy pastoral islands, the parking lot is such a potent and recognizable spatial form. So easily and often maligned, perhaps the most redeeming aspect of the impossibly vast retail parking lot layout, common in so much suburban and exurban American sprawl, is its adaptability.

Of course, the desolate corners of the many off-hours strip malls and shopping centers lend themselves to a range of social and antisocial applications. But given the potency of our shared cultural connection to automobiles and the heroic autonomy they are famed for providing, along with the comforting regularity of efficiency and order, it makes sense that these spaces seamlessly accommodate so many experiences of everyday life beyond just parking.

On any weekend in the San Fernando Valley, for instance, there are any number of car shows, some hosted by small clubs of enthusiasts and appreciators sitting in lawn chairs around a few restored Corvettes in the parking lots of vintage burger joints or cafés, and others that are more formal affairs, with entry fees, celebrity autograph booths ("Meet Danny Trejo!"), and musical acts, all spread out across high school parking lots throughout the Valley. More pragmatically, big-box hardware chains, like Lowe's, have a penchant for relegating some sector of their sprawling parking lots to material storage, as overflow lumber yards, or in the springtime, to accommodate the sudden influx of fresh shrubs and flowers ready for planting from the garden center.

A shopping mall down the road from us—one of many "brick and mortar" retail centers struggling from the current omnipresence of Amazon and its lesser online shopping alternatives—has ceded the massive corner parking lot of a vacated anchor behemoth like Macy's, Sears, or Lord & Taylor, to serve as storage for construction equipment. Strikingly, among the slumbering excavators, bulldozers, and dump trucks, the empty space has also been given over to groups of massive component pieces of precast concrete roadways and bridges. Here, the defunct consumer excesses that necessitated acres and acres of overflow parking are now quiet, contemplative sculpture parks. Instead of the hustle and bustle of shoppers, shopping carts, shopping bags, and

... store employees, these spaces play host to a neat, massive line of knock-off Richard Serra sculptures, almost certainly fabricated overseas and floated across one ocean or another to rest patiently in this mostly deserted suburban corridor.

No matter the context, it seems these disregarded corners, ostensibly intended to accommodate automobiles, are fated to accumulate clutter and other questionably permitted storage. In the outskirts north of Rome, on the grounds of the Foro Italico sports complex, a quiet section of parking lot provides a home for a misplaced chunk of travertine, buffered by a pen of construction fencing. Ironically, the startled looking eyeball is almost the exact size of a car. It's frustrating that this apparently inevitable outcome—of poetic, meditative contrast amid the chaos of parking and reversing cars—so rarely seems to play a significant role in cultural depictions and imaginings of the built landscape. ❄

❄ For a welcome exception, see the use of parking lots and parking garages as important settings and set-pieces in the films of Joel and Ethan Cohen, especially Fargo (1996, PolyGram Filmed Entertainment).

> “ It was being gradually borne in on me by Rome that one of the vital things that make a great city great is not mere raw size, but the amount of care, detail, observation, and love precipitated in its contents, including but not only its buildings. It is the sense of care—of voluminous attention to detail—that makes things matter, that detains the eye, arrests the foot, and discourages the passerby from passing too easily by. And it goes without saying, or ought to, that one cannot pay that kind of attention to detail until one understands quite a bit about substance, about different stones, different metals, the variety of woods and other substances—ceramics, glass, brick, plaster, and the rest—that go to make up the innards and outer skin of a building, how they age, how they wear: in sum, how they live, if they do live. An architect's flawless ink-wash rendering of a fluted pilaster surmounted by a capital of the Composite order is, necessarily, an abstraction. [...] It has not become architecture yet, and it will really not do so until it is built and the passage of light from dawn to dusk has settled in to cross it, until time, wind, rain, soot, pigeon shit, and the myriad marks of use that a building slowly acquires have left their traces. Above all, it will not become architecture until it is clearly made of the world's substance—of how one kind of stone cuts this way but not that, of bricks whose burned surface relates to the earth below it. Now Rome—not the society of people in the city, but

… their collective exoskeleton, the city itself—is a sublime and inordinately complicated object-lesson in the substantiality of buildings and other made things, in their resistance to abstraction.”

▲ Robert Hughes, Rome: A Cultural, Visual, and Personal History (New York: Alfred A. Knopf, 2011), 10.

--- 👂 ---

▲ **Charismatic megaflora**

While the creeping spread of the not-so-living "living green wall" (the name itself positively vibrates with a sense of barely repressed ecological threat) seems to have an outsized impact in hotel lobbies and the occasional corporate office interior, finding such a "green wall" under assembly in the otherwise institutional entryway of a historic greenhouse conservatory on Chicago's West Side, of all places, strikes a discordant tone.

We spent an afternoon lurking in the lobby, trying to seem nonchalant, while observing with rapt fascination as a disinterested facilities staff member opened bag after bag of dried lichen, hot-gluing each green, spongy wad to the wall, working his way outward from the fire alarm. After the project was complete, we couldn't help but marvel, taking in the newly created miniature landscape. Your vision wanders around the periphery of the surface, and your eyes can start to give you the impression of an altered perspective, as if hovering at low altitude over a charmingly, even-tinted forest, like you had been levitated upward by magic, or perhaps by a helicopter.* The stubborn impropriety of the fire alarm, which seems blithely unaware of its disruption of the scene, can easily be redacted by closing one eye and holding up a thumb to blot out the offending object, and suddenly the forest seamlessly reemerges.

* For a cinematic example, see: the opening title sequence of The Shining (1980, dir. Stanley Kubrick, Warner Bros.).

--- ❁ ---

▲ **Holding pen**

▲ The contemporary use of the term “quarantine" derives from the Italian quadraginta, “for forty days,” the amount of time ships were required to wait in the harbor before being permitted to offload their cargo.

There’s something delightful in the capacity for language to synthesize a discrete meaning simply through the expression of a grouping (“forty

... days" comes to stand for something much more weighty and complex). Quadraginta sounds benign enough, yet "quarantine," as a term, feels so cold—round and then tinny to the ear. Similarly, "fortnight" derives from "fourteen nights," which seems intuitive enough, but then the word always clangs a bit in hearing it, perhaps due to the awkwardness of it referring to multiple days, yet specifically ending with the singular of night. Then there's "biweekly," which, along with "biannual," stubbornly and bizarrely resists offering a reliably consistent meaning.

--- ⃠ ---

▲ **Find-and-replace warehouse**

We're accustomed to the idea of one document overwriting another document in digital space, or that different versions of information will sit on top of, or exist in fuzzily close proximity to other versions.

Hunting through dozens of versions of files, each appended "-FINAL," is a familiar hassle. But this phenomenon only occasionally manifests itself in reality. Most new buildings and renovations remove any indication of the previous or go to great lengths to emphasize continuity. It could be more creatively and intellectually enriching to imagine the world as a cluttered Desktop or a delightfully unregulated 3D Warehouse, where new and old are in a less polite relationship but are instead in messy, if unintentional, opposition: the 10 versions of the building in different stages of development, different modes of resolution, and different levels of quality, just blithely stacked on top of one another. Although it has its roots in construction issues, the crux of this architectural problem developed symptomatically at the junction of two walls, at the limits between the flatness of the elevation and its conceptual confrontation with material thickness. Out of this junction, one can read architecture's registration of societal customs, attitudes, and values, just as published arguments often aimed at an "appropriate" way of doing things, rather than simply a definitive solution.

▲ **Immersive signage**

▲ With their formal restraint and single-minded emphasis on the clarity of presentation, traffic signs are the most fervently a-stylistic visual communication elements one can find in the built environment.

Because of their impeccable uniformity, along with the banal circumstances in which we encounter them, it's easy to regard these flat, aluminum polygons as simply concomitant with the surrounding landscape. Mixed

... in among the trees and bushes residing along the highway, they seem an inevitable presence in the scrolling scenery that rushes past us, rather than an intervention upon it. It's almost as if the placement and appearance of NO PARKING and SPEED LIMIT signs were dictated by something primordial, like the functions of mitochondria and ribosomes, rather than the standards and specifications of traffic engineers and work crews. Because of their reliance on simple shapes and colors, road signs tend to evoke the formal language of children's toys. And seen up-close, they're always larger than you imagine them to be, which is an inevitable side effect of the compressive power of speed on our perception of the world. In those rare instances when you might pause to consider a road sign as a discrete, designed object—usually in a decontextualized circumstance, like when used as kitschy decoration in a rumpus room or parlor—it's the overall scale, the largeness of the lettering, and the vibrancy of the color treatments that strangely defamiliarizes the overall object. You can occasionally stumble across historical road signs installed by private auto clubs and made redundant decades ago by state and federal codes. These ancient artifacts seem similar to their standardized, contemporary descendants, yet strangely unfamiliar, adorned with AAA logos and quirky, mid-century lettering. You might find such relics tucked away near the quiet summits of some serpentine hillside streets in neighborhoods of East Los Angeles, like Mount Washington or Monterey Hills.

Broadening the scope, we can also look beyond graphical modes of communication and consider strategies that influence motorists' behaviors through spatial interventions. Rather than passively communicating a precaution or law, there is the class of material interventions aspiring for "traffic control." When a SPEED LIMIT sign doesn't do the trick, speed bumps and speed humps are enlisted to entice drivers to slow down. While their names may seem interchangeable—perhaps just a variation in regional dialects like "soda" versus "pop"—these are actually two distinct devices that use different gradations in form to apply force, or the threat of force through dramatic bouncing, in an attempt to moderate vehicle speeds. Similarly, rumble strips, which sometimes go by the more dreamy nickname "sleeper lines," are a smaller scale roadway deformation. These miniature undulations on the surface are like those snaking ribbons of wind-formed sand ridges you might see across a desert landscape, only tidier. Of course, rumble strips are not only a material manipulation of the road surface, but in turn, a manipulation of the interior

1 The more novel installation of rumble strips as "singing roads" provides a pleasant but disappointingly superficial proposition for an alternate reality; one in which transportation infrastructure and public thoroughfares could occasionally be lively, engaging, and playful, rather than just myopically functional. While only a few examples exist in the U.S., one prominent installation was purpose-built for a 2008 Honda commercial, then subsequently removed to address the noise complaints of neighbors and rebuilt nearby. The stretch of the "Civic Musical Road" in Lancaster, California inflicts a vibration on passing vehicles that vaguely resembles a portion of Rossini's "William Tell Overture." For a portion of the driving ...

... environment of the vehicle itself. The sense of invasive interruption following a momentary dalliance onto a section of rumble strips at the edge of the highway is impressively jarring. Their purpose, after all, is to startle a distracted or dozing driver to refocus their attention, compelling them to correct the course of their vehicle back onto the safety and familiarity of smooth pavement.

Perhaps this newly proposed traffic sign classification, the example of "immersive signage" shown here, represents an increasingly plausible, even urgent type of roadway intervention. It exists somewhere between graphic communication and spatial form. It's an onomatopoeia of traffic signs in that it attempts to not only didactically explain but to materially enact instructions to drivers. Or perhaps it is the latest civilian-initiated Federal Highway Administration experiment for the kind of signs which will inevitably be required when we all start careening around in flying cars.

--- ---

... public, this recognizable orchestral snippet might evoke memories of hoofbeats and galloping horses in "The Lone Ranger," while for others, it may be synonymous with "Looney Tunes" shorts, or zany scenes in television sitcoms. While the connection between the overture itself and the surrounding landscape is far from obvious, perhaps these associations to popular culture provide the rationale to connect the famous herald of trumpets with its environs in the exceedingly quiet, desolate expanses of the Antelope Valley. Unfortunately, the translation from road surface to tires to vehicle frame to automotive interior to human ear leaves a lot to be desired. In this particular incarnation, it's perhaps the most fleeting example of "sight-seeing," or rather "sound-hearing," that one could possibly imagine.

§ 7 - Complex problems often require simple answers, while simple problems sometimes result in excessively complicated, circuitously constructed, and surprisingly fussy fixes. The relentless, unforgivable, and inflexible nature of the built environment produces responses in the form of **edits** that often take the path of most resistance.

▲ **Vestigial fountain**

“ Grata la voz del agua /
a quien abrumaron negras arenas [...]”

▲ Jorge Luis Borges, “Alhambra,” Borges: Selected Poems, ed. Alexander Coleman (New York City: Penguin Books, 1971), 395.

Although a small city in the San Gabriel Valley claims to be its namesake, the more appropriate complement to the Alhambra palace in Granada is found on the opposite side of the Verdugo Mountains, smack-dab in the middle of the San Fernando Valley. Along a retail strip just west of the Van Nuys airport, mixed in among stores selling home furnishings and automotive parts, you will find a 25,000 square foot warehouse, the façade of which is completely covered in a dense tangle of ivy.

Thanks to the generous archival efforts of Google Street View, we can rewind the storefront over a decade and observe the progress of the creeping vines, beginning on the north side of the building and moving steadily southward, year after year. As you click through this digital documentation of captured growth, you can watch the ivy making patient progress across the stucco until the most recent image, in which the building itself seems to be formed entirely of verdant green leaves and entangled branches. It's as if the entire warehouse was painstakingly pruned and snipped exclusively from flora, creating a boxy topiary of a retail storefront. This enchanting façade sets the tone as you pass through the entryway to find yourself immediately overcome with the ecstasy and exuberance of over 500 decorative garden fountains gurgling, spitting, splashing, and sloshing in the dreamlike central Valley warehouse showroom: you have entered Reseda Discount Pottery & Fountains! The humidity in the room stands at about 110 percent, and the moisture clings to your skin at once. A series of uncomfortably narrow aisles—laden with sopping wet, bright green utility mats—carve the large space into three lengthy sections.

When you encounter fountains in the "wild," say in a garden or a courtyard, they are always fulcrum points, central and spatially distinct from everything around them, in a sense isolated. To see them here in the showroom densely arranged with such unrelenting redundancy is especially remarkable. The effect is similar to the effortless enchantment that Chris Burden achieved by tightly arranging another familiar form in the built environment, the otherwise commonplace street lamp. And just as with street lamps, fountains simply aren't installed in groups, so the novelty of this gesture feels radical. Here in the showroom, masses and combinations of

See: § 6, "Machine vision eye test" (pg. 140-143)

See: Chris Burden, Urban Light (2008), Los Angeles County Museum of Art.

Note: Argumentatively inclined readers will be tempted to counter that the William Mulholland Memorial Fountain in Los Feliz, designed by Walter S. Claberg and dedicated in 1940, is a possible rebuttal to our claim concerning the lack of landmark fountains in Los Angeles. While it certainly leverages authority by virtue of memorializing the region's most famous water systems engineer, any claim to notoriety as a popular destination isn't supported by evidence: one struggles to find, for instance, a postcard or a famous film scene centered on the Mulholland Fountain. Historically, a strong claim could have been made for the recognizability of the central fountain in Pershing Square,

… clashing decor and contrasting styles are everywhere: the refined filigrees of three-tiered bronze fountains are next to a miniature ersatz rocky waterfall painted in strangely hyper-natural tans and sandy highlights. There are massive urn-like enameled bubblers and modernistic, infinity-edged box fountains in black granite, polished stainless steel, and glass. Of course, there is an endless array of cast concrete cherubs, eagles, frogs, turtles, and lion heads. The rear of the showroom is dominated by a six-foot-tall bust of Buddha. Ribbons of water delicately drift down the enormous visage on all sides, issuing from a bubbler in the ushnisha oval on the crown of the head.

While the sight of all this decorative ostentation is noteworthy, the acoustic quality of the showroom is, in fact, the most immediately stunning aspect of this space. Whereas most American cities count at least one recognizably famous public fountain as part of their retinue of tourist attractions, they are extremely rare in Los Angeles.❣ Add to that, the unfamiliar sensation of hearing hundreds of simultaneous streams, drips, and jets of water—usually a calming and delicate sound, but downright disorienting when experienced in mass. Rather than one cohesive, focused roaring of water, it's the ambiguous and disembodied quality of the aural effect that is remarkable: an all-encompassing white noise like 500 television sets tuned to different varieties of black-and-white fuzzing static. Finally, and most obviously, is the fact that we're accustomed to encountering water features in the diffusion of outdoor space. The simple but effective gesture of cramming all of this frenetic sensation and stimulus indoors is what propels the experience from the realm of the merely uncanny to the stratospheric limits of the sublime.

The Andalusian Alhambra and the adjoining Generalife gardens convey a veneration of water through material and spatial expression, organizing the compound around a series of generous fountains, channels, cascades, and reflecting pools. The remarkable abundance of water on the Iberian Peninsula, compared with North Africa's deserts to which the Moors had been more accustomed, explains this impulse to architecturally focus the space around the circulation and display of water. The San Fernando Valley offers its own landscape of hydrological icons, manifestations of a wishful invocation for the abundance of water; for instance, the head of the Los Angeles River, which takes form at the confluence between two streams in Canoga Park, the Donald C. Tillman

… designed by Johan Caspar Lachne Gruenfeld in 1910, had it not been removed during the 1952 scheme to cram a parking garage beneath the square. Otherwise, Ricardo Legorreta's abstracted, purple aqueduct from the 1994 Pershing Square renovation seems to be enjoying a popular reassessment, a benefactor of both the revitalization of Downtown and the rejuvenated cultural credibility of postmodernism.

❣ ☼ See: § 4, "Show-off" (pg. 106-108). Ben Hooker first introduced us to the glorious experience of the Reseda Discount Pottery & Fountains showroom.

... Water Reclamation Plant in Van Nuys, the nearby Sepulveda Dam, and the Los Angeles Aqueduct Cascades in Sylmar.➥ We advocate for an addendum to this index of sites: to include the echoing interior showroom of Reseda Discount Pottery & Fountains.✪ This point of interest is a critical destination for anyone looking to better understand the rising sense of anxiety and compulsively opulent display of water abundance in a region increasingly stricken by drought and the myriad of knock-on calamities that proceed drought conditions, most potently among them, devastating wildfires. In particular, this gallery showroom of landscaping decor provides a compelling perspective on how consumer culture gives form to the generalized dread that has been self-inflicted on a society unwilling to seriously respond to climate change, resource mismanagement, and callous waste.

--- ⌑ ---

▲ **Suture**

The Toyota Camry is so ubiquitous on American roadways as to be almost completely unnoticeable. This is especially true of the Camry XV10 series, marketed from the early- to mid-1990s.

The enormous popularity of the Camry throughout this era seems to have been especially felt on the streets of Los Angeles. Japanese manufacturers were still riding the explosive wave of popularity for compact imports in America, due to the trauma inflicted by the 1970s oil crises, along with the supply shocks and ongoing gasoline price increases thereafter. The economic demands of an average 32-mile daily commute in Southern California in 1991 were motivation enough for many Angelenos to abandon any sentimental attachment to inefficient and less reliable domestic models, embracing the apparent future of globalized car manufacturing. While the Sony Walkman and Panasonic boombox may have been more symbolically potent icons of international manufacturing and trade—particularly for their attachment to American popular culture (one of the reciprocal currencies of globalization)—consumer electronics aren't quite as intimately connected to the everyday mythology of American life as the car. In a sense, these early imports were "brand ambassadors" for globalization on the streets, with their happy, unaggressive logos and branding, coupled with progressive, vaguely futuristic names like Civic, Altima, Miata, Supra, and Sentra. And throughout the 1980s, many of those overseas competitors to the American market were building large production facilities throughout the U.S., giving rise to an emphatic narration in television commercials to "meet the North American built Toyota Camry!" The ubiquity, coupled with its apparently indefatigable engineering, means that the mid-1990s XV10 Camry is still a regular presence, lining the curbs and driveways of neighborhoods throughout Los Angeles today. Like a piece of street furniture—a bus bench, a fire hydrant, or a trashcan—it doesn't so much reside on the roadway, as it seems to constitute the street itself. Although this remarkable anonymity was certainly not the intention of its designers and marketers, it is nevertheless an extremely impressive status for an automobile to achieve.

"Toyota Camry," Wikipedia. [https://en.wikipedia.org/wiki/Toyota_Camry].

Cheryl Collier and Torben Christiansen, "The State of the Commute in Southern California," Transportation Research Record, No. 1338 (Transportation Research Board: 1992), 73, web [http://onlinepubs.trb.org/Onlinepubs/trr/1992/1338-010.pdf].

Betamax King, "1995 Toyota Camry Commercial," YouTube, Sep. 8 2018 [https://www.youtube.com/watch?v=xZS1yO1ChjY].

See: § 3, "Community beautification" (pg. 90-91).

The infinitely patient, slow, steady force of tree roots and plant stems—and the resultant rending, shifting, lifting, and fracturing of roads and sidewalks they're able to inflict—is positively disquieting. By extending the variable of time, these apparently inanimate, languorous tendrils are capable of impacting the built environment in a manner that resembles, in thumbnail, the promised devastation an inevitable seismic catastrophe would inflict on the entire region.

The scariest part about being in an earthquake isn't necessarily the shaking, but rather not knowing if the event is just getting started or almost over. In the destructive thrusting of tree roots, the process itself is imperceptibly slow, but the eventual outcomes are impressively tectonic. The evidence of the stoic, unrelenting labor of trees is clear as you walk—or attempt to walk—down the slanted and cracked slabs of sidewalk near any mature Indian Laurel Fig, particularly in much of Hollywood and Downtown Los Angeles. Their smooth, white trunks are usually decorated with carved initials and spray-painted tags, and the entire base of the tree is often covered with a few layers of rolled-on gray graffiti abatement paint. Casting our view down to the tree's base, where the layers of paint give way to dirt and concrete, the subcutaneous flexing of lateral roots have shrugged the slabs of sidewalk upward at radical angles, creating ledges six inches or taller and exposing hollows and gaps beneath the concrete that seem ideally suited as a domicile for rats or other rodents. If it's still present at all, the adjacent curb will shove out into the street. Web-like tracings of buckling rifts in the asphalt are often visible, stretching out into the roadway itself. The city placed a compelling price tag of $1.3 billion on all of this ad-hoc

... editing of the cityscape by its unruly plant inhabitants.✂ It is an insurgent defacement of the city by the flora. Most people would be arrested if they went around taking a sledgehammer to city sidewalks⚒—particularly if their efforts resulted in a $1.3 billion repair bill! But the trees get a preemptive pardon because they do it very slowly.

✂ See: Damien Newton, "L.A. Finally Shamed Into Doing Something About Decrepit Sidewalks," Streetsblog Los Angeles, Apr. 2, 2015, web [https://la.streetsblog.org/2015/04/02/l-a-finally-shamed-into-doing-something-about-decrepit-sidewalks/].

⚒ See: Veronica Rocha, "Man Charged After Destroying Donald Trump's Walk of Fame Star with Sledgehammer," Los Angeles Times, Nov. 17, 2016, web [https://www.latimes.com/local/lanow/la-me-ln-charges-donald-trump-star-sledgehammer-20161117-story.html]. See, also: Nardine Saad, "Trump's Walk of Fame Star Smashed Again, This Time by Someone Dressed as The Hulk," Los Angeles Times, Oct. 2, 2020, web [https://www.latimes.com/entertainment-arts/story/2020-10-02/trump-walk-of-fame-star-smashed-incredible-hulk].

> " The fact is, that each time there is a movement to confer rights onto some new 'entity,' the proposal is bound to sound odd or frightening or laughable. This is partly because until the rightless thing receives its rights, we cannot see it as anything but a thing for the use of 'us'—those who are holding rights at the time. [...] There is something of a seamless web involved: there will be resistance to giving the thing 'rights' until it can be seen and valued for itself; yet, it is hard to see it and value it for itself until we can bring ourselves to give it 'rights'—which is almost inevitably going to sound inconceivable to a large group of people. The reason for this little discourse on the unthinkable, the reader must know by now, if only from the title of the paper. I am quite seriously proposing that we give legal rights to forests, oceans, rivers and other so-called 'natural objects' in the environment—indeed, to the natural environment as a whole."
>
> ▲ Christopher D. Stone, "Should Trees Have Standing?—Toward Legal Rights for Natural Objects," Southern California Law Review 45 (1972), 455-456.

◀ Pruning a tree or a bush is one of those landscaping chores that is conceptually clear but evokes a mild sense of anxiety for the unpracticed hand when the time comes to pick up a pair of shears and carry out some manipulation on the landscape around us.

Of course, consulting a horticulturist or arborist, or simply hiring a landscaper, is a quick shortcut to forego this uncertainty. There are billboards for tree service companies peppering the roadways as we run errands and acquire lawn tools at the various hardware stores in the area. Landscaping and tree trimming are among those vocations, along with plumbing and heating and cooling services, which seem the most inclined to

... employ cheesy puns in their company names, like "All Trees Under the Sun." This is almost certainly because such services are difficult for consumers to distinguish and because new clients mostly garner referrals from neighbors or family. Therefore a pun, no matter how cringe-worthy, is an obvious aid to memory, and the more inane the reference, the more memorable.

Note: This phenomenon is epitomized by the prevalence of landscaping services whose company names make reference to Blade Runner (1982, dir. Ridley Scott, Warner Bros.), a film that couldn't be any less related to lawn care. But the clumsy obviousness of the pun seems to make it a favorite for entrepreneurs across the country. The first page of search results on social media reveals landscapers doing business under some variation of "Blade Runners" in the outskirts of cities including Boston, Orlando, Atlantic City, and Washington, D.C., as well as in Guyana and Austria. We can't help but wonder how many of these company's founders have watched the film. If, as we suspect, the answer is "not many," then it's a testament to the poetic resonance of sci-fi author Alan E. Nourse's title, which was taken for the film, even though "blade running," like lawn care, has absolutely no relationship to the movie's plot; See also: Abraham Riesman, "Digging Into the Odd History of Blade Runner's Title," Vulture, Oct. 4, 2017, web [https://www.vulture.com/2017/10/why-is-blade-runner-the-title-of-blade-runner.html].

Despite our trepidations, we've thought about pruning a few of the smaller trees around our own house. We tell ourselves that such interventions are necessary to more assertively regulate the tree's shape, condition its growth, and design its outcome. But there's a certain hubris that goes along with pruning, a sense that humans are helping trees in the process, that we know better than they do. Strangely, most of the trees around us that call for some trimming are at least as old as we are. In the case of the more intimidating specimens requiring professional intervention—from people with hard hats, harnesses, chainsaws, and scissor lifts—the tree is certainly older than anybody carrying out the work and quite possibly older than the ages of the entire work crew combined.

Who are we to exert any control over them? We're still just getting to know their names. Among those who are still with us:

- ★ Gran Abuelo, a 3,600 year-old Patagonian cypress (Fitzroya cupressoides) who lives in Chile
- ★ Methusaleh, more than 4,800 years old, a Great Basin bristlecone pine (Pinus longaeva), who lives in California (the United States Forest Service protects the exact location)
- ★ Sarv-e Abarkuh, about 4,500 years old, a Mediterranean Cypress (Cupressus sempervirens) who lives in Iran
- ★ Jōmon Sugi, a Japanese cedar (Cryptomeria japonica) who lives on Yakushima in Japan, whose age isn't verified, but might be more senior than all at 7,200 years old

If pruning is a collaborative effort, meant to be a mutually enriching exchange between humans and plants, it's increasingly clear we're not bringing enough to this shared project.

--- ✂ ---

▲ **Utilitarian supergraphics**

It's peculiar to see measurements transcribed onto a building surface. Why should something so self-evident need attention called to it? This turns architecture itself into a measuring device, a tool for its own evaluation.

See: The facade of the architecture practice James R. Doman and Associates, designed and painted by the firm in the 1970s;
See also: Mel Bochner, Measurement Series, in particular Measurement Room, 1969, Galerie Heiner Friedrich, Munich.

Seeing the built environment like this produces a moment of cognitive dissonance, as measuring in this way becomes an immediate task of self-interrogation. One can't help but wonder: "Is that really four feet, three inches long? It can't be. It looks longer than that! That's gotta be more like five feet! Or at least four-foot-seven! Well, wait, how tall am I again?"

> "And when I hold the ruler against the table, do I always measure the table, might I not sometimes be checking the ruler?"
>
> Ludwig Wittgenstein, quoted in Bernhard Leitner, The Wittgenstein House (New York: Princeton Architectural Press, 2000), 16.

Whereas design pedagogy and architectural practice expend so much energy venerating the final architectural form, the mockup is a structure created as a matter of course—a necessary byproduct to be processed and moved past, to be mistreated and abandoned, if not destroyed outright.

It is an ancestor of the building that it ultimately models, which exists to expose the faults and substantiate the tolerances of the intended outcome. Its doppelgänger status comes from its adherence to life-size proportions and material fidelities, a condition embedded in the word's origins: mock, from the Old French mocquer "to deceive, make fun of, deride, jeer," possibly derived from the Middle Dutch mocken "to mumble" or Middle Low German mucken "grumble," which is perhaps simply imitative of such speech. Or, most provocatively, possibly from the Vulgar Latin muccare, "to blow the nose," which derives from the Latin that we still recognize: mucus. ✷

✷ See: "Mock," Online Etymology Dictionary, web, [https://www.etymonline.com/word/mock].

▲ **Clipping mask**

▲ Every time we find ourselves confronted by the decaying remnants or scattered debris of the built environment, we face some uncomfortable cognitive hazards.

... Anybody who has experienced the vocational misfortune to find themselves laboring away on a demolition project—as we have at points in our lives, though blessedly rare as they may be—had to reckon with a glaring and stubborn absurdity that the process reveals about everyday life: the insistence that all architecture is permanent and necessary. We see this hubristic perspective characterized in the routines of contemporary design and building practices in the United States where the consensus has mostly settled on the position that we, as designers and builders, have little or no obligation to seriously consider any of the deeper implications of construction beyond the ideal performance of the building and its systems for the immediate client. The U.S. Green Building Council advocates for sustainable building practices and modestly ambitious reuse goals, but the USGBC would never deign to suggest that many projects obviously should not be undertaken or that many buildings do not need to be built. At the same time, in the midst of a punishing and ongoing housing crisis in most major urban centers, advocacy groups are woefully outmatched by misdirected NIMBY-ist regulatory stasis and the biases of staggering economic inequality. For institutions like the USGBC, and particularly the American Institute of Architects, the status quo of building and construction is unassailable, with perhaps minor adjustments and improvements made around the margins. As such, we propose the formation of a U.S. Non-Building Council.

When it comes to superficial fixes and improvised design interventions, the most interesting choices and installation details can always be found in transitory spaces.

See: § 1, "Bold lashes" (pg. 40-41).

Mixed in among the otherwise humdrum atmosphere of retail surplus on store shelves and the routines of consumer exchange at checkout counters in so many convenience stores, airports, and fast-food chain restaurants, the quirkiest improvisations in material finishes are always certain to reward scrutiny. Given the monotonous corporate uniformity and joyless, antiseptic pragmatism that characterizes such interiors, these moments of exception always stand out for their stubborn and slightly subversive tendency to capture the sense of serendipity and agency inherent in their making. Whether it be a fussy notch hacksawed out of a length of crown molding to accommodate a light fixture at a Subway franchise location, or two trim plates stacked on top of each

... other perpendicularly in a fruitless, but formally enigmatic attempt to conceal an electrical junction box in a bodega, these formal manifestations reveal a point of friction between finish and fidelity.

A central consideration in this phenomenon is the lowly cultural status of these liminal spaces. The endless extraction of natural resources and churning circulation of capital both animates these sites and specifically attenuates our capacity to recognize and interpret them. The workers in these places, themselves rendered utterly invisible by careless and unsympathetic class systems and economic structures, are the only ones subjected to these surroundings for extended lengths of time. The stakes are set incredibly, delightfully low when it comes to surface finishes. It's as if the interiors themselves were treated as invisible by their corporate caretakers; fast-food dining areas and terminal gate lounges are seen merely as sluices and spillways for the endless circulation of never-ending capital. Add to that the constraints of standardized component parts from which these incidental elements are typically assembled, and the accompanying likelihood of narrow craft expertise (in most cases) for the laborers involved in the construction and maintaining of these spaces, and a sort of excessively limited but endlessly expansive improvisation becomes the norm. Reminiscent of the popular "There, I Fixed It" meme,☺ where the toolset and the material palette to draw from are shallow, solutions will inevitably present themselves when a piece of the building needs repair, but almost always with charmingly quirky results: like so many disposable Band-Aids® for architectural finishes.

☺ See: "There, I Fixed It," Cheezburger Network [https://failblog.cheezburger.com/thereifixedit].

▲ Stubborn attachment

▲ A multitude of objects we encounter on a day-to-day basis are noteworthy particularly because of the measures taken to make them secure. For instance, the anonymous ballpoint pen that's apparently been stolen one-too-many-times from the local post office. It's now irreversibly and dramatically attached to the counter with a short length of small gauge ball chain and at least a half-roll of packaging tape. The pen is completely mummified in tape, rendered almost entirely unusable. It is no longer so much a courtesy supplied by the post office as it is a physical manifestation

… of the ongoing anxiety and friction caused by patrons' insensitive thoughtlessness in constantly pocketing the politely provided writing implement.

Every additional layer of packaging tape conveys an escalating sense of exasperation. We can almost hear the frustrated clerk sighing and unspooling another layer of protective tape around the pen, mumbling the phrase, "This is why we can't have nice things!"

And one can't help but take note of the surprising number of anti-theft steering wheel locks used to secure modest-looking early-1990s sedans in so many Los Angeles neighborhoods.Ⓟ In a city whose layout and infrastructure largely excludes any feasible transportation options other than the automobile, it's understandable that so many Angelenos will resort to such theatrical measures when their livelihoods depend on access to a car. The blunt, cumbersome industrial styling of The Club® on car steering wheels serves as an embodiment of understandable desperation and distrust pervading so many neighborhoods throughout the city. In areas like Hancock Park or Brentwood Park, these stage props for security theater take the form of miniature placards mounted on sticks situated curbside near ornate gates and imposing security walls. Usually hexagonal with red and blue color schemes, these signs seem to be groping for some invocation of authority and intimidation, with vaguely bureaucratic combinations of lettering like ACS, ADT, POST, WT, or the suspiciously generic Security Service Systems.📹 Some of the most lavish properties will include multiple security company signs, placed at intervals across the frontage, the way that ornamental stones, boxy Cedar shrubs, or undulating mounds of mulch might be strategically arranged in rhythmic punctuation. In this way, enforcement measures and the performance of security become another decorative signifier—along with the landscaping—meant to carefully simulate the variety and disorder of nature, but nevertheless, convey a sense of control and containment. Inevitably, the true intention of these security signs is spelled out directly beneath the company logo: "ARMED RESPONSE." The explicit threat of violence is always present, but in keeping with the precepts of affluent domestic styling, it is whispered rather than screamed. Even the logo graphics of these signs reflect this preference for subtly: rather than icons of burglars,♟ badges, or handguns, they tend toward eagles, flags, or houses.

Ⓟ See: § 7, "Suture" (pg. 161-163).

📹 A quick internet search for "Decoy Security Signs" provides a wealth of alternatives to actually paying a home security company for services.

♟ See: "Boris the Burglar," National Neighborhood Watch, National Sheriffs' Association, web [https://nnw.org/logo-usage].

... This ecosystem of security landscaping and surveillance technology has increasingly given way to the antiseptic, frigid coldness of glossy "smart" doorbell cameras, like the Google Nest Hello or the Ring Video Doorbell.▮ With their HAL 9000-esque glowing circle oculi, ultra-wide-angle fields of vision, enhanced digital zoom, endless alerts to paired devices, and the ability to harness cloud-based facial recognition algorithms, these products bundle ubiquitous, ever-present monitoring into the existing vocabulary of the neighborhood. Rather than industrial-grade locks, ornamental steel bars, or threatening yard signs, this "new neighborhood watch" ⊙ barely calls attention to itself at all. We recently purchased a "non-smart," non-surveillant doorbell and discovered that today's entire product category of doorbells simply mimics the "smart" aesthetic. While hoping to resist the urge to participate in the "Panoptification" of the semi-public residential space of the sidewalk, front yard, and porch, all of the burdensome associations activated in the formal language of "smartness" are increasingly unavoidable. In the not-too-distant future, every single doorbell, welcome mat, mailbox, porch light, planter, and garden gnome—the whole coterie of public-facing domestic accessories—will be "smart," networked, and surveillant. And if not, every object will be doing its best to masquerade as such.

> "The writing of miniaturization does not want to call attention to itself or to its author; rather, it continually refers to the physical world. It resists the interiority of reflexive language in order to interiorize an outside; it is the closest thing we have to a three-dimensional language, for it continually points outside itself, creating a shell-like, or enclosed, exteriority. 'Correctness of design' and 'accuracy of representation' are devices of distance, of 'proper perspective,' the perspective of the bourgeois subject."
>
> ▲ Susan Stewart, <u>On Longing: Narratives of the Miniature, the Gigantic, the Souvenir, the Collection</u> (Durham, NC: Duke University Press, 1993), 45.

--- ❢ ---

⊙ See: § 3, "Handrail vistas" (pg. 92-94).

▬ See: Drew Harwell, "Doorbell-Camera Firm Ring Has Partnered With 400 Police Forces, Extending Surveillance Concerns," <u>The Washington Post</u>, Aug. 28, 2019, web [https://www.washingtonpost.com/technology/2019/08/28/doorbell-camera-firm-ring-has-partnered-with-police-forces-extending-surveillance-reach/].

▲ **Dormer smear**

▲ The empty space that stretches across a gabled roof, in between two protruding dormers, is often a site for modest home additions. The architectural outcome of this renovation strategy leaves the dormers embedded at the opposite ends of the add-on space, like two bookends to a section of wall, almost

… as if each side of the two dormers were subjected to a cartoonish rubber-stretching effect to account for the void between them.

This pragmatic approach to home renovation is so rewarding for the casual passerby because it provides a friendly, recognizable gesture, like a finger pointing in the direction that we should direct our attention, as a means to access an understanding of the house's various permutations over time. This is why online galleries of historical photos are such reliably consistent features on social media and in the "clickbait" ad sections of so many popular news websites. We've all spent a few cheerily brainless moments scrolling through a "listicle" of historical photos that have been overlaid onto their present-day settings: for instance, a 1965 Richard Avedon portrait of Bob Dylan glumly posing on the rain-soaked hexagonal pavers of Fifth Avenue, overlaid on top of a sunny color image of the present-day portion of Central Park, the images positioned to align the saplings at the edge of the park in the 1960s with the mature American Elms in the contemporary color image. Of course, in this case, the interest is easily attributable to the subject matter: a celebrity musician captured by a famous photographer situated on an iconic stretch of the Upper East Side. But the phenomenon of overlaying and aligning provides a visual gesture that clearly and compellingly bridges the cognitive distance between the past and the present.

Ironically, just across Fifth Avenue from where Avedon captured Dylan, we can find a helpfully uncooperative example of architectural additions expressing a clear connection to an existing form.❖ In the designed environment—and especially in the often disregarded expanses of residential building types—the sense of interest and satisfaction this legibility elicits is particularly potent because such a perspective is so rare. Legal frameworks, building codes, and epistemologies have a strong bias for decisive beginnings and decisive endings. The designed objects and buildings around us work hard to clearly assert a sense of finish in their form and presentation—they each embody a stable and sturdy sense of doneness. In the case of the humble Cape Cod dormers, the addition is noteworthy because it happens to keep the gabled form of the existing architectural elements painstakingly intact. Once there were two dormers, now there is one extraordinarily wide dormer. Like the pelvic bones and femurs found in some marine mammals, which provide evidence of the long arc of evolution, the formal recognizability of the dormers

See: Anna Gragert, "Overlapping Photos Merge Historic Scenes from the Past with the Present," My Modern Met, Oct. 18, 2015, web [https://mymodernmet.com/nick-sullivan-double-take/].

❖ See: the Gwathmey Siegel addition to the Solomon R. Guggenheim Museum, New York, 1992.

See: St. Louis Public Radio, "Pruitt-Igoe Implsion," YouTube, Sep. 11, 2009, video, 1:08 [https://www.youtube.com/watch?v=738WpY2_JV8].

... turns them into vestigial organs of a home addition. Thinking about the hips of whales and dolphins can be a particularly helpful opportunity to consider an individual specimen as part of a larger phenomenon. Rather than simply an aberrant, redundant organ, we can look at these instances as indicators of both past and impending transition. The dormers provide us with an architectural asterisk, pointing toward modularity in domestic space that has largely been eschewed in American building practices. Here, the dormers ask the question: how far can we push this cultural tolerance in residential vernacular? Where is the boundary between the in-progress and the incomplete?

> “I am an ephemeral and not too discontented citizen of a metropolis considered modern because all known taste has been evaded in the furnishings and the exterior of the houses as well as in the layout of the city. Here you would fail to detect the least trace of any monument of superstition. Morals and language are reduced to their simplest expression, at last!”
>
> ▲ Arthur Rimbaud, “City (Ville),” Illuminations and Other Prose Poems, trans. Louise Varése (New York: New Directions, 1957), 57.

A helpful international counterexample is the polykatoikía, the phenomenon of “unfinished” construction, which has been particularly attributed to Greece. This building practice challenges commonly held simplistic ideas of what it means for a living space to be “complete.” Such houses are intentionally left with empty levels of exposed structural steel or scaffolding as if awaiting an imminent component that may never arrive. While dismissive postings on travel forums and various derogatory articles proffer explanations about tax schemes or unpermitted buildings, a more reasonable explanation suggests the practice as a manifestation of a more adaptable posture in relationship to time, form, and finish. These architectural vacancies are left exposed to maximize the ease of inevitable future additions, anticipating the eventual arrival of new children, or of aging parents moving in with their children.

See: Nicola Szibbo, “Landscapes of Abundance... or Debt & Decay?” The Urban Fringe Blog: Berkeley Planning Journal, Oct. 22, 2013, web [http://ced.berkeley.edu/bpj/2013/10/landscapes-of-abundanceor-debt-decay]; See also: Melanie A. Crane, “Uniquely Crete... (What the Brochures Won't Show You),” Cretan Chronicles Blog, Jul. 14, 2010, web [https://cretanchronicles.wordpress.com/2010/07/14/uniquely-crete-what-the-brochures-wont-show-you/].

§ 8 - The instances in which we observe the strangely satisfying catharsis of Things **Fitting** Perfectly Into Other Things are few and far between in the built environment. Endearing strategies of connection falling short of total unity are far more prevalent. The perfect fit is often one not seen; as the unity between discrete elements reaches such a high degree, one object is nearly indistinguishable from another.

See: The wonderful Tumblr at [https://thingsfittingperfectlyintothings.tumblr.com/]

▲ **Flatten all layers**

▲ Given their long history relative to other functional building components, it's no surprise that window shutters reflect such a variety in their design and distribution throughout the world. From mitigating the sun's light and heat to providing a durable barrier against high winds, their ongoing status as a requisite symbol of domestic stability is reflected in their capacity, harkening back to a time when houses demanded almost constant attention, maintenance, and routine upkeep from their occupants.

✱ See: § 7, "Dormer smear" (pg. 178-180).

... Along with the most immediately pressing chores that were replaced by plumbing and heating systems—tending to wood stoves or coal boilers, or bringing fresh water in and wastewater out with buckets and pans—the everyday task of opening and closing window shutters based on the weather is today made redundant by double-paned, argon gas insulated residential window systems.

The most interesting and least considered piece of hardware in the shutter assembly is the hinge mechanism. The apparatus that allows them to swing, to move between states of open and closed, also effectively changes their status from one of barrier and containment, to one of storage and display. The hinge exists between the two, where use and signifier are in limbo. When window shutters are not "in use," they are decoration; as insulated vapor barriers and double-paned window systems render them redundant, their decorative position becomes permanent. As with many vestigial components,✱ this can often give way to a confusion of statuses and meanings. It's common to see shutters that barely fit the windows to which they've been paired: the narrow sliver of shutters placed on either side of an enormous picture window or at the end of an extended horizontal sweep of ribbon windows. The decision to trim a section of fiberglass stone veneer quoining to accommodate the shutter provides a delightfully charged collision between competing symbolic and material logics. Ultimately, it appears that the shutter has taken precedence by virtue of layering—as with digital bitmap workspace, the element on the top layer collapses and eliminates all information beneath.

See: § 1, "Bold lashes" (pg. 40-41).

With the increasing glut of home automation systems and networked, smart home devices, the symbiotic relationship between people and buildings will be eminently eliminated. As with automobiles, the contemporary home is now a product instead of an ongoing project, an inscrutable black box suffused with sensors and microprocessors that preclude any possibility of consumer augmentation beyond those permitted in the "settings" or "control panel." The window shutter calls back to the era when upkeep was more demanding and menial but also cast occupants as caretakers and attendants of the building. As with those cylindrical LED table lamps—made of semi-opaque plastic to capture the glowing aura of a bedside candle, even offering modes of carefully programmed dimming and flickering patterns dictated by some tiny microprocessor concealed within—the non-functioning window shutter meagerly gropes in the direction of domestic traditionalism.

... As a once essential sheltering component of the home exterior, the stubborn stoicism of today's mass-produced, bolted-in-place vinyl shutter mounted to either side of so many windows in suburbs across the country is a vestigial affectation, merely a visual accent.

--- ---

▲ **Trompe l'fire marshal**

The quirkiest applications of prosaic interior details—such as trim plates, molding, ventilation covers, fire egress signs, and strobe indicators for people with hearing impairments—are found in transitory spaces like convenience stores, airports, and fast-food chain restaurants.✪

✪ See: § 7, "Clipping mask" (pg. 172-174).

Conversely, places that self-consciously assert some historical affinity or make dubious claim to their cultural dignity—as in the Getty Villa, Hearst Castle, or the Huntington Library—are also brimming with bizarre accents and fittings. In attempting to resolve surface finishes in the least obtrusive way possible, the insistent pragmatism of visual restraint can reveal surprisingly unexpected associations and outcomes. Mounting a green, fire egress "EXIT" sign so that it perfectly aligns to a painted frieze, seamlessly straddling the corner of a trompe l'oeil entablature, suggests a totalizing logic of organizational unity. It offers a moment of promise to those of us mildly inclined towards obsessive compulsion, who find immense satisfaction in sorting, organizing, and labeling. It suggests that the unmitigated chaos of visual stimuli and apparently disjointed details that catch our eye could be clarified and find their place through some simple act of arrangement and alignment.

> "The fake-Italian look – that's definitely the number one thing people hate."

Daveed Kapoor quoted in David Zahniser and Roger Vincent, "Geoffrey Palmer Seen As Both Downtown L.A. Trailblazer, Steamroller," Los Angeles Times, Dec. 8, 2014, web [https://www.latimes.com/local/cityhall/la-me-palmer-empire-20141209-story.html].

--- ---

▲ **Landscape seams**

> “Also amazing was, laying there on my gut, I was able to observe very slowly some grass, on a blade basis! And what I found was, each blade is its total own blade, they are not all exact copies as I had always thought [...]. No, each blade had a special design of up-and-down lines on it, plus some blades were wider than others, and some were yellow, with some even having little holes that I guessed had been put there via bugs chewing on them?”

George Saunders, “Jon,” in In Persuasion Nation (New York: Riverhead Books, 2006), 55-56.

The effort many people devote to their foliage, flowers, shrubs, and bushes is a labor of nurturing and sustaining a collection of living organisms: the plant life surrounding our homes. Opting for artificial turf changes much of this work into an effort to simply maintain something mechanically produced, not nurtured and grown.

Instead of watering, edging, fertilizing, weeding, mowing, trimming, and cutting, the synthetic yard demands a type of upkeep that is less attached to the ambition to nourish and encourage natural growth, but something more akin to hobbyist collectors: to maintain a product in “like new” condition. Rather than cultivating life, yard work instead focuses on maintaining the perpetual sameness of a factory-produced surface as much as possible. Installed artificial lawns are occasionally brushed or sprayed clean, and eventually removed to make way for a replacement covering. The typical lifespan for an artificial lawn is 25 years. In many cases, the turf may be subject to a product warranty or some other guarantee of satisfaction. Turning a natural span of lush, grassy lawn into a petroleum-based, facsimile consumer product, reflects almost perfectly on the ambition of the very yard work it makes redundant. After all, the yard is a space where wildness is denatured, brought under strict control for the appreciation of the property owner and curb appeal.

The American lawn is a public display of control, stability, and ambition. The more fussily agonized and excruciatingly

… finished the detail, the more the property owner's mastery of the landscape is asserted, and with that the suggested mastery of social and professional realms of life.

As the changing environment impacts the accessibility and abundance of resources—fossil fuels, plant habitats, and freshwater reserves—it's worth considering what cultural practices need to be radically altered or done away with altogether. Is a natural grass lawn worth the threat of depleted aquifers? Are facsimile yards worth the expenditure of fossil fuels? Or would we be better off fundamentally rethinking the organization and distribution of the built environments around us?

For an earlier and extended version of this text, see our essay "A Taxonomy of Synthetic Turf Patent Drawings," POOL, web [http://www.pool-la.com/besler-and-sons-turf]; See also: Ian Besler, "The Meticulous Engineering Behind Your Neighbor's Fake Lawn," Gizmodo, May 15, 2015, web [https://gizmodo.com/the-meticulous-engineering-behind-your-neighbors-fake-l-1703956730].

> "To [Geoff] Thran, his replica Rose Bowl is an annual art project, an ode to the game he loves. He likes to do it all himself, starting with the right fonts, then tracing the logos themselves by flashing them against his garage wall. […] 'I just kind of get my stuff at OSH,' says Thran, 45. […] It's a beautiful thing really, a little quirky, a tad obsessive, ridiculously inventive."

Chris Erskine, "An Expert in His Field, He Creates His Own Rose Bowl and Super Bowl," Los Angeles Times, Dec. 3, 2013, web [http://www.pressreader.com/usa/los-angeles-times/20131204/282467116691660].

\- - - - - -

▲ **Privatized sidewalk**

▲ The chain link fencing that surrounds so many vacant lots, construction sites, and intentionally neglected public resources—like fountains, playgrounds, and restrooms—weaponizes the pliability of the "temporary" as an implicitly benign status in the era of brutal and unremitting neoliberal austerity.

Along with its close cousin, orange PVC mesh netted fencing, chain link fencing is anonymous, conveying informality and a lack of precision or long-term intention that other types of fences—say the white picket, the dog-ear, or the wrought iron fence—would elicit. This anonymity is useful

… for the cruelty and violence free market ideologies enact on built spaces around us. As an alternative to the obscenely blunt material measures of spikes, studs,✳ razor wire, or boulders,⊗ these comparatively softer measures turn to less evocative, more permissible languages of material form, such as planters, tilted benches, and the apparently temporary imposition of chain link fence corridors, enclosed on all sides, spanning city blocks for hundreds of feet to unjustly, and at times illegally, prevent the emergence of "homeless encampments." Of course, such measures represent only a small fraction of the encroachments and interventions on public rights and interests by private entities in the effort to maximize property values at the cost of making communities less open, less accessible, and less public. Whether these assaults on public space and people play out through the "re-sorting" of demographics in neighborhoods by way of gentrification or obstructive legislative action, the inequities and impacts fall on the least protected communities. As with any designed intervention in public spaces, the most charged outcomes happen at the edges between propriety and jurisdiction, where regulation or the harsh monotony of precedent haven't asserted any control.

✳ See: § 1, "Deterrent studs" (pg 30-31).

⊗ See: "Mysterious Boulders Appear on West LA Sidewalk As Apparent Deterrent to Homeless Encampments," <u>ABC7 Eyewitness News</u>, Sep. 10, 2020, web [https://abc7.com/sidewalk-boulders-mysterious-mystery-los-angeles-homeless/6416394/].

For one account of the ways individuals and businesses deploy callous, unjust, and illegal measures in order to make public space unhabitable in the wake of civic failures at the city and county level, see: Benjamin Oreskes, "Desperate To Get Rid of Homeless People, Some Are Using Prickly Plants, Fences, Barriers," <u>Los Angeles Times</u>, Jul. 10, 2019, web [https://www.latimes.com/local/lanow/la-me-ln-homeless-encampment-planter-fence-resident-neighborhood-20190710-htmlstory.html].

> "After work at city hall, I walk home on straight, flat sidewalks. Their lines converge ahead of me into a confusion of trees and lawns. […] The sidewalk is four feet wide. The street is forty feet wide. The strip of lawn between the street and the sidewalk is seven feet. The setback from curb to house is twenty feet. […] This pattern—of asphalt, grass, concrete, grass—is as regular as any thought of God's."
>
> ▲ D.J. Waldie, <u>Holy Land: A Suburban Memoir</u> (New York: W.W. Norton Company, 2005), 48.

- - - - - -

▲ **Dental retainer door handle**

▲ No recent development in visual culture has done more to hasten the oncoming, beguiling collision between city and simulacra than the spread of relatively cheap, large-scale vinyl sticker graphics.

High-resolution prints of hamburgers the size of sedans and gyros as big as sleeping bags adorn almost every viable customer-facing surface on

... storefronts across the city. When hand-painted signage and advertising fell out of use, it was only a matter of time before printing technology—electrostatic and piezoelectric inkjet processes—advanced sufficiently to allow for the reproduction of high-resolution imagery at relatively affordable prices. AA

The timeline of this visual innovation maps almost perfectly with the turn of the century, the apex of the dot-com bubble, and the emergent fantasy of the oncoming hyper-commodification of every surface and resource imaginable. In the summer of 2000, newspapers and local news broadcasts were inundated with stories promising that any automobile owner could forfeit the exterior surface of their car for the use of revolving advertisers in order to earn additional income. The repeated marketing slogans promoted by each vinyl auto-wrap company reinforced the idea that converting unproductive private property into a rentable display space could generate enough income to partially or even entirely offset auto loan payments, insurance coverage, and gasoline costs. This brief frenzy of journalistic attention quickly subsided; still, the example offers an early precursor of the phenomenon that technology companies like CouchSurfing, Uber, Airbnb, Lyft, JustPark, and many more would eventually formalize as the "sharing" and "gig" economies. As such, vinyl graphic wrapping is a cornerstone example of the vacuous and barely obscured grift characterizing the vast majority of technological innovations since the World Wide Web first commodified: Novel, disruptive innovations promise additional income, flexibility, and freedom, but in practice, only bring more financial precarity and social inequity.

The idea of a highway where every vehicle is a billboard, turning roadways into a panoply of colorful slogans and commercial incitements—the traffic jam as a commercial break—is mildly compelling. As with so many speculative futures and superficial utopias Silicon Valley plunged us into, the early invocations and imagined implications are never quite as contained as we collectively imagine. If anything, the past decades have revealed how deficient our imaginations can be in considering the knock-on effects and downstream costs of disruption.

- - -] - - -

AA See: § 2, "☹ ☹ ☹" (pg. 55-57).

See: Roy Rivenburg, "Advertisers Have Got Us Covered," The Los Angeles Times, Jul. 7, 2000, web [https://www.latimes.com/archives/la-xpm-2000-jul-07-cl-48822-story.html];

See also: Rodney Ho, "Several Start-Ups Are Wrapping Cars in Advertisements: Drivers May Get Paid or Free Use of a Vehicle, but a Group Sees 'Ad Creep,'" The Wall Street Journal, Jun. 6, 2000, web [https://search.proquest.com/historical-newspapers/several-start-ups-are-wrapping-cars/docview/1932154907/se-2?accountid=13313].

§ 9 - Self-conscious instances of showiness lend a sense of personality, even swagger, to the otherwise prosaic or banal objects and spaces we encounter every day. An **ostentation** can be both the unforeseen consequence of a synthesis of parts over time, or the result of an isolated and self-aware decision by a single author.

▲ **Perrenials**

▲ Since its debut on the residential landscape in the late 1970s, the satellite dish has made a remarkable journey from precious technical apparatus to banal functional element.

Like periscopes emerging from submarines, satellite dishes are a point of connection, a fragile orifice offering mediation and connection between a cordoned and regulated interior environment and the messy, unregulated outside world. As with the spindly, skeletal armature of aluminum rooftop antennae,✉ the satellite dish can be a piece of decorative flair for the house—a visual accent for the exterior, like a brooch or a corsage pinned

See: § 7, "Gable louver antenna access" (pg. 164-166).
See: § 2, "Palm tree" (pg. 50-52).
See: § 2, "Utility palm" (pg. 72-74).

... to the neckline of a gown. In the contemporary landscape, we commonly see technology and communications equipment operating less as ostentatious status indicators and more as mundane, disregarded elements, no longer vaunted but simply left to mix in with their surroundings. Over the past five decades, the satellite dish has made this pitiable journey from Space Age wonder to prosaic flora: muted gray and black clusters of Dish Network and DirecTV saucers hang precariously from the edges of apartment balconies, like ferns or petunias blooming out of planter boxes, or they hold vigil in the suburban backyard among the isolated dogwoods and other saplings. In their approximation of the natural landscape, it's as if they are trying to become one with the flowers, shrubbery, and trees. The manufactured environment is entangled more and more with what we traditionally conceive as "natural," blurring any meaningful distinction between the two. This narrative parallels our own personal and intimate relationship to technology, as touchscreens, apps, and algorithms mediate our lives more comprehensively each day. As such, the satellite dish offers an object lesson for conceptualizing the steady, inexorable process of technological transition, from something clearly discrete—in which the boundaries between one and the other are totally legible—to one that is almost entirely integrated, with blurry and amorphous edges that are constantly in flux.

> " Television is the software of the earth. Television is invisible. It's not an object. It's not a piece of furniture. The television set is irrelevant to the phenomenon of television[...] 'Television,' says video artist Les Levine, 'is the most obvious realization of software in the general environment. It shows the human race itself as a working model of itself. It renders the social psychological condition of the environment visible to the environment.'"

▲ Gene Youngblood, Expanded Cinema (New York: Dutton Paperback, 1970), 78.

▲ Screen fatigue

“We can exclude that the ‘like’ came from the Holy See, and it has turned to Instagram for explanations.”

▲ A Vatican spokesperson quoted in Angela Giuffrida, “Vatican Asks Instagram How Pope’s Account Liked Photo of Brazilian Model,” The Guardian, Nov. 19, 2020, web [https://www.theguardian.com/world/2020/nov/19/pope-francis-instagram-like-brazil-model-natalia-garibotto].

Just about anything displayed using an LED matrix is imbued with both an expressive voice and the mesmerizing ability to captivate vision.

After vending a bottle of Diet Coke with a thud into the dispenser bay at its base, a text readout on a soda machine will encourage you to “ENJOY!” with glowing blue text scrolling across the narrow display at a jerky pace, letter-by-letter. It feels charmingly dystopic: both a forceful directive and a cheery farewell. The machine’s casual appropriation of impersonal filler phrases underlines the meaningless affectations punctuating everyday social interactions. A laser cutter in the fabrication lab displays a cheery “HELLO!” on its LED display panel when it starts up, including the exclamation point! The seven-segment lettering display has a tendency to be slightly italicized, which makes it read all the more emphatically.

Carl Kinsley patented the seven-segment display in 1903 as a method to make telegraph messages more legible. The ubiquity of LCD and LED readouts during the ensuing decades imbued this typographic style with a sense of voice and consciousness that heralded the oncoming machine era. With the boom of digital electronics in the 1980s, nearly all of the devices regulating daily life used some variant of Kinsley’s display: bedside alarm clocks, train and bus route signs, car radios, gasoline pumps, wrist watches, pocket calculators, and VCRs. The visual clarity of the glowing numerals, and the anxiety they provoke, is cinematically conveyed in any dramatic development involving ticking time bombs. The seven-segment display will soon be consigned to the lowly status of a skeuomorph: an empty formal gesture used to evoke nostalgia.

These machinic affections have also made their way into the realm of spoken salutations, like when the sensor system regulating the swing-arm gate at the parking garage determines that your parking pass is valid. “HAVE A NICE DAY,” it intones flatly as the horizontal plastic arm lifts skyward, “DRIVE SAFE.” The rhythm and cadence are never quite comfortable, always sounding a bit strained or hurried. Still, the idea that we can find social nicety, comfort, or even higher meaning through digital displays, text-to-speech language processing, and inscrutable algorithms is increasingly common in contemporary American culture. An evangelical prophet quoted in a recent interview compared his spirituality to the pervasive idea that mobile devices are constantly surveilling our conversations in order to serve more lucrative advertising messages into our social media feeds: “God works the same way,” he proselytizes, “he’s listening to everything you say.”

Examples of spirituality grappling to find meaning amid the infinitude of digital chatter include straightforward forums like askmoses.com and rabbiwithanswers.com, to various personal guidance and reflection softwares, such as Confession: A Roman Catholic App, which received the first known imprimatur for an app. More tangible examples are available as well. The televangelist Joel Osteen™ sells an Inspiration Cube™ for $39.99, offering a fixed playlist of audio tracks that cycle at the push of a button: sermons, affirmations, and inspirations. It can also be used as a general-purpose Bluetooth speaker, which begs the question whether this device confers any spiritual

… value on the immense range of idolatrous music it could then be made to broadcast.

See: Mike Killion quoted in Ruth Graham, "Christian Prophets Are on the Rise. What Happens When They're Wrong?" The New York Times, Feb. 11, 2021, web [https://www.nytimes.com/2021/02/11/us/christian-prophets-predictions.html].

See: Tim Drake, "First iPhone App to Receive an Imprimatur," National Catholic Register, Jan. 28, 2011, web [https://www.ncregister.com/blog/first-iphone-app-to-receive-an-imprimatur].

See: "Joel Osteen™ Inspiration Cube™ - Be Inspired Anywhere, Anytime!" website, n.d. [https://www.inspirationcube.com/].

--- ---

▲ **Camouflage-ish**

Painting a camouflage pattern on an automobile certainly seems like a reasonable goal for a "Weekend Warrior." But, as many know from personal experience, when it comes to D.I.Y. tasks and amateur efforts, intentions and outcomes can often be woefully mismatched.

An infamous example of this phenomenon is Ecce Homo (c. 1930) or "Ecce Mono," the fresco in Borja that was woefully altered in 2012 by local volunteer Cecilia Giménez in a good faith attempt at amateur art restoration (what the church diplomatically referred to as "una intervención" on her behalf). ★ Applying a camouflage pattern to a pickup truck is a similarly ill-fated "intervention." One can't help but feel empathy for the ambitious and aspirational spirit evident in both cases, a spirit that turns out to be doomed by overconfidence. Just as touching-up the colors on an old fresco seems, deceptively, like a simple act of tracing, the extemporaneous camouflaging of a truck is easy to visualize in the mind, but that ease resists a simple translation to pigments and surface. Camouflage is both vague and specific. We can recognize camouflage when we see it, yet we would almost certainly struggle if asked to create our own visual approximation without the benefit of a reference pattern or guide. Judging from the repetition of the forms, the intervention here was produced using a stencil, but a stencil of what exactly?

See: Elías García Martínez, Ecce Homo (c. 1930), Santuario la Misericordia, Borja, Spain; and also see: Cecilia Giménez, Untitled ("Ecce Mono"), Aug. 25, 2012, Santuario de Misericordia, Borja, Spain.

★ See: "Un hecho incalificable," Centro de Estudios Borjanos, Institución Fernando el Católico, Aug. 7, 2012, web [http://cesbor.blogspot.com.es/2012/08/un-hecho-incalificable.html]; See also: Raphael Minder, "Despite Good Intentions, a Fresco in Spain Is Ruined," The New York Times, Aug. 23, 2012, web [https://www.nytimes.com/2012/08/24/world/europe/botched-restoration-of-ecce-homo-fresco-shocks-spain.html]; See also: Doreen Carvajal, "A Town, if Not a Painting, Is Restored," The New York Times, Dec. 14, 2014, web [https://www.nytimes.com/2014/12/15/world/a-town-if-not-a-painting-is-restored.html].

▲ **Doric affirmation**

◀ The formal expression of security—the use of architecture to regulate space not only functionally but formally—is an ever-escalating confrontation of resources that will demand increasingly radical tactics as economic disparity and housing instability continue to increase.

The gated sequestration of marginal spaces, like entryways and egress points, gives rise to a brutally adaptive streetscape. For example, take the rolling metal shutters reserved for use as blunt and anonymizing overnight security barriers on retail fronts in neighborhoods like the Jewelry District and the Fashion District at the southeastern periphery of Downtown Los Angeles. These metal slats are coiled-up inside a cylinder above the door frame during daytime hours and are unfurled with a characteristic racket to mark the close of the business day. They are less an architectural barrier than medieval armor. They have a remarkable capacity to alter the texture of the streetscape—sidewalks crowded with racks of retail goods, stacks of mannequins, PA equipment blaring dance music from DJ party equipment stores, and wholesale kitchen supply dealers—into vacant canyons punctuated by parking meters, fire hydrants, and the tents of the unhoused. The housing crisis across the country and the shameful neglect that all gentrifying cities have inflicted on their most vulnerable and increasingly unhoused residents is framed as an exception to the claimed ideals of free-market capitalism, supposedly an outcome of the limitations of bureaucracy and the ineffectualness of welfare intervention. But any serious consideration reveals such injustice is repeatedly the intended outcome—its visibility is the only detail that free-market advocates wish to avoid.

“ Although Ruscha uses the adjectives ‘hideous’ and ‘passé’ to describe the buildings, he clearly recognized the potential cultural value of including them in a widely distributed book.”

▲ Virginia Heckert, Ed Ruscha and Some Los Angeles Apartments (Los Angeles: The J. Paul Getty Museum, 2013), 31.

- - - 🏛 - - -

▲ **Weird fungus**

> "A family in Pomona says that their house is being consumed by fungus and their insurance company has denied their claim to repair it. Chris and Crystal Zettell discovered a strange substance in their home that was turning the wood to mush, KTLA reports. Chris described the fungus as an 'an orange pancake-batter-looking ooze.' The couple tried to scrape the ooze away in December, but it soon returned. Crystal told KTLA that the couple had ten people come and check the ooze out, but no one seems to know what it was. Finally, the Zettells did their own research and determined it is something called 'Merulipora incrassata,' a wood-eating fungus known as 'The House Eating Fungus.'"

Juliet Bennett Rylah, "A Family's Home Is Rapidly Being Eaten by Fungus," LAist, Jun. 16, 2015, web [https://laist.com/2015/06/16/fungus_eats_house.php].

It's worth putting too fine of a point on what is otherwise an arbitrary observation: Satellite dishes bear an uncanny resemblance to a cluster of oversized mushrooms bursting out of a building facade.

It's easy to imagine them as purely decorative accents in certain arrangements like you might find at some ramshackle fairytale theme park. Of course, why anyone wants a visual association to fungus mounted on their apartment—except as a purely pragmatic necessity to receive more television channels—is difficult to reconcile. But when we consider the extraordinarily narrow range of options available for residential decorations, this observation suggests one possible strategy for opposing the crushing conservatism of outward expression that social mores around homeownership generally dictate to be tactful and acceptable.

These same restrictive social mechanisms lend subversive potency to regularly occurring memes that cast gawking derision on the irregular or unexpected interior design details circulated on social media from property listing sites like Zillow and Trulia. These real estate platforms are insufficient at capturing the sense of permitted, snoopy, invasive curiosity that makes "Open House" visitations so deviantly compelling. The unfortunate viral tendency to ridicule the tastes and

… comforts of some anonymous home seller—someone who decorated their living room with hundreds of porcelain dolls, or their kitchen with Disney merchandise, or their bathroom with deep shades of purple, or their bedroom with paintings of cats—provides a digital facsimile of similar compulsions.

To lesser or greater extents, every neighborhood or town seems to have its own particular examples of specific eccentric decor or outlandish gesture. Growing up in the Chicago suburbs, a neighbor caused an uproar one spring by reusing an old toilet as a decorative planter in their front lawn—both the bowl and the upright tank overflowing with yellow tulips and purple crocuses in bloom. The planter was subsequently removed within a few weeks. In Los Angeles, the "House of Davids" on the west side of Hancock Park served this role. Like all great contemporary mythology, what makes these anecdotes resonant is each of us have witnessed a different version of it.

These instances of formal rebellion in the domestic built environment are each their own litmus tests of "taste," a way of surveying the boundaries of propriety and acceptability within the fraught and oftentimes obtuse social dynamics of microcommunities, and the handful of neighbors through whom we structure our perceptions of the deplorable and the desirable.

- - - ✿ - - -

See: Nick Gerhardt, "The 30 Most Ridiculous Real Estate Listing Photos," Family Handyman, Mar. 20, 2019, web [https://www.familyhandyman.com/list/the-30-most-ridiculous-real-estate-listing-photos/].

See: Nita Lelyveld, "A House That Claimed His Fame," Los Angeles Times, Mar. 21, 2014, web [https://www.latimes.com/la-me-house-of-davids-20110816-story.html].

The Edgy Bit

Jonathan Jae-an Crisman

> “ There’s nothing I like more than when, for example, there’s been a near-disaster at NASA and they say: ‘If it hadn’t been for the chewing gum…’ It’s not because I want to fetishize chewing gum or the aesthetics of gum pressed over some break or membrane; it’s because we have the intelligence to think: ‘Hey, there’s a malleable, mastic material and we can use that.’”
>
> ▲ Richard Wentworth, Interviewed by Kevin Henry. In “Parallel Universes: Making Do and Getting By + Thoughtless Acts (mapping the quotidian from two perspectives),” presentation at College Art Association, 2007.

I assume the position, the embodied shape so common to contemporary life, reclining on the sofa, head tilted just up enough to see my smartphone held by one hand, my thumb flicking through an endless stream of Instagram images. I stop at one, posted by @ianbesler: a square image of an awkward building detail, a handrail that does an overwrought little dance to get around an ill-placed column. The image sticks with me. It is funny! But also endearing, and kind of impressive? Who was the unnamed creator behind this striking design detail?? Would a standard-issue starchitect ever be so bold??? The image, one of many, debuted on the now-defunct @ianbesler account and has since joined many more in Best Practices. It shares an ineffable quality with a range of other architectural moments, varying from mysteriously incongruous doors leading who-knows-where, to two-dimensional window decals on dentist offices that perfectly (horrifically?) cut and frame massive teeth. This quality is explored elsewhere in the architecture and design practice of Besler & Sons—co-founded by Erin Besler and Ian Besler—who find generic rain gutters and how-to videos more interesting than whatever is on the cover of this month’s Architectural Record. In their words, they are “expanding the definition of architecture through active participation with amateur creators.”

The theoretical lineage of their practice can be traced to ideas of the everyday, breathing new life into our otherwise dated

... understanding of the concept within architecture. Sociologist Henri Lefebvre, who first pointed toward the possibility in analyzing the everyday in his text Critique of Everyday Life, described it as "the reverse side of all praxis." ↻ Which is to say, the processes that emerge outside of disciplined method to "get the job done," necessarily performed as a sophisticated guesswork or even formed out of a superconscious autopilot. Returning to that little handrail boogie, one can track the Beslers' interests precisely with the handrail's accomplishment outside of disciplinary structures. Architecture, improbably, cannot lay claim to this minuscule moment's sparkle. What does looking at this handrail do for us? Lefebvre helpfully notes that the "critique of everyday life encompasses a critique of art by the everyday and a critique of the everyday by art." Does this mean that the image is the art, critiquing the everyday? Or is the handrail, itself, the art, putting on blast a masochistic Besler & Sons who engage in a type of autocritique? Of course, this all suggests that art is decidedly not part of the everyday, and vice versa. In another image, a generic four-inch steel column majestically blasts through asphalted eaves—sublime.

Lefebvre's emphasis on critique does not fully capture how to read these images. I would suggest that the magic of that handrail and its ilk first begins to emerge when the everyday itself is understood as art. The Beslers' practice is one of observing, engaging with these moments, and soliciting them for membership in the club of Architecture, pointedly inquiring, "do you want to participate in this thing we do?" Further, the image of a dancing handrail is not merely an object of its own accord, but it points toward a subcontractor who had to figure out how to get the handrail around the damn column: an unfolding of events that sparked a moment of creative intervention. There is an everyday practice there, embodied not only by the handrail, but also by its maker. When we shift our frame of reference in this way, from the everyday generally to everyday practice specifically, we can get more explicit about the images in Best Practices because practice is necessarily both embodied and emplaced. Each image exhibits a "making do," as described by sociologist Michel de Certeau, or what he refers to as a bricolage—a tactical reaction in the built environment in creative and subversive response to the strategic praxis of Architecture. The closest translation to this French loanword is probably "DIY"—apropos for the practice of Besler & Sons, who

↻ Henri Lefebvre, Critique of Everyday Life (Volume 2): Foundations for a Sociology of the Everyday, trans. John Moore (London: Verso, 2002), 43.

Lefebvre, Critique of Everyday Life, 19.

Though another example of how to read such images could include Robert Venturi and Denise Scott Brown's reduction of the everyday to the semiotics of postwar American consumer culture in "Signs of Life: Symbols in the American City," the 1976 exhibition at the Renwick Gallery of the Smithsonian American Art Museum.

Michel de Certeau, The Practice of Everyday Life, trans. Steven Rendall (Berkeley: University of California Press, 1984), 29, 174.

… have explored elsewhere in their work the extravagant contemporary descendants of de Certeau's proto-DIY. And for de Certeau, "making do" certainly seems to be both art and everyday practice; he describes it as something made of "artistic tricks" and—perhaps even more intriguing—that which involves a particularly "improper" approach to getting things done. In Best Practices, we are forced to contend with the artistic nature of what might otherwise be dismissed as trickery or misuse.

As for the emplaced nature of the images, while they have come from several different places, their origin is Angeleno. Is there something specific about Los Angeles and bricolage? De Certeau's use of the term came out of his observations in Brazil, France, and New York, among other places, suggesting that this delightfully subversive activity can happen—and, in indeed, must—in any place around the globe. Where there is power, control, design, there is always the bricoleur getting in through the backdoor. Of course, the cultural specificity of everyday practices varies by geography. One key source of inspiration in Los Angeles is what urban planner James Rojas refers to as "Latino urbanism," highlighting the rasquache tactics found in front yards, murals, and other sites where someone has made do. ✍ This aesthetic ethos was celebrated in the Chicano Art Movement and the Beslers also point toward its alchemic approach to art, place, and life, turning nothing into something. There are obvious moments, like in an image of a borrowed signal box cover used to fashion a planter, and less obvious moments in which the more active construction images reveal the invariably Latinx construction worker upon whose unseen labor this makeshift metropolis relies.

There is the rare wink or a joke at the bricoleur's expense in the images: "look here, one chump sealed off their floodlights with paint!" (Or maybe our bricoleur is enacting some civil disobedience against a nasty landlord, and we just don't know the full story?) But for the most part, amateur hour is celebrated by Besler & Sons because of its wit and verve. Artist Richard Wentworth describes the part of our brain making everyday practice happen as "that very edgy bit of our intelligence." ⬇ Indeed, some of these moments can only be described by their synchronicity with high-powered computational tools, a cage fit here or a content-aware fill there. This "edgy bit" is all too often dismissed by high culture, praxis, and

✍ James Rojas, "Latino Urbanism in Los Angeles: A Model for Urban Improvisation and Reinvention," in Insurgent Public Space: Guerrilla Urbanism and the Remaking of Contemporary Cities, ed. Jeffrey Hou (London: Routledge, 2010).

⬇ Richard Wentworth, interviewed by Kevin Henry, in "Parallel Universes: Making Do and Getting By + Thoughtless Acts (mapping the quotidian from two perspectives)," presentation at College Art Association, 2007.

... conventional expertise, despite being the one bit holding everything together. The Beslers' practice of seeing, archiving, and classifying these moments is more difficult than one might imagine. The everyday, by definition, floats outside the grasp of discipline. To engage with amateur creators requires an always "on" field scan of the built environment, a sophisticated pattern recognition capturing the delightful moments that escape the rarified world of Proper Channels. ✓ The Beslers see the art of the everyday in the least expected places, the geographies excluded by discipline.

✓ Artist Stephen Johnstone calls this "the poetics of noticing." See "Introduction: Recent Art and the Everyday," in The Everyday, ed. Stephen Johnstone (Cambridge, MA: MIT Press, 2008), 18.

The outsider nature of this practice becomes inverted—perhaps it turns "improper," to use de Certeau's language—in one of my favorite images depicting a high-culture corner moment at the Getty Villa. The embodiment of architectural power if there ever was one, the Getty holds one of the largest endowments of any arts organization in the world, the Villa its shrine to Western civilization, renovated for over a decade by architects Machado and Silvetti at the turn of the 3rd millennium. But, even here, someone had to figure out where to place that interloping exit signage and fire alarm! Both are color coordinated with the surrounding trompe l'oeil fresco, giving a splash of continuity to the classical patterns in red, green, and white. It's a nice reminder that no matter how rarefied the air may be, at the end of the day, in our moments of greatest shame and pride, we're all just trying to make do.

Builder Conversations

In late 2020 Fiona Connor conducted a series of interviews with people who give shape to the built environment.

November 7, Aida
(b. 1981)

How did you learn your trade?

I started when I was really young. My mom doesn't have that preconception of certain boundaries for women and men, she was always the person around the house fixing things and cutting wood and fabricating patios, you know. She didn't restrict herself. I was the person who helped her with all that stuff, so I learned a love and desire for making really early.

I went to art school to be a painter, but in that process, I started to make my own stretcher bars because I just couldn't afford to buy them. I realized there was something really therapeutic about going into the shop and being very physically involved in the making of something for hours. After realizing how much I enjoyed it, I basically begged them to give me a job in the shop even though I knew I was highly unqualified for it. I started working in the shops at Otis College of Art and Design in 2005, and within like two-and-a-half years, I went from part-time tech to manager of the shop. I've been manager ever since, and the shop's grown a huge amount.

Do you ever do other work or projects outside of your job in the shops?

Probably for the first eight to ten years that I worked in the shop, there was never a moment when I was not doing a commission for someone. I don't really do side jobs for people that much anymore, just because I feel like I don't have the energy. But I was always doing fabrication for artists, building furniture for people, framing things, doing installations. In 2012, I bought my own house in Westchester, and the first week, my cousin, who is a contractor, my boyfriend at the time, and I fully gutted the whole house. It's been a long eight-year process.

Is that where you live now?

I'm in Westchester, yeah. It's a really cute, quiet street, and the area was not affected by the crash that badly, which is why I wanted to buy a house here. I basically bought one of the worst houses in the neighborhood and am slowly trying to put it back together. We totally gutted it; we tore out the ceilings, took down the walls, pulled out all the plumbing, all the electrical, everything. We redid all the framing of the interior. It's a really stressful way to live because you're basically living in a construction zone and everything you own is in a Tupperware bin since there's nowhere to put anything.

There were a couple of years where there was no heating; in the first year, there were no lights, everything was just a floor lamp. I wasn't fully aware of what it would be and how long it would take me, especially since I wasn't anticipating my boyfriend at the time to leave. And so, for a while, it was just me in the house building everything by myself, and because I was working at Otis, it was just like nights and weekends. Progress was slow. But I wouldn't trade it. I've learned so much that I wasn't expecting to have learned. For a lot of the people I talk to home ownership is a little bit intimidating, and when they do buy homes, they get stuck in this money trap of trying to always pay someone else to come in and fix things when they go wrong. I know every single inch of this house, so if and when things happen, I know exactly how to fix it.

What does "best practice" mean to you?

The one thing I will say is I didn't pull permits on any of it. I wish that I had pulled permits. I have friends who work for the permitting office and everything. I think just for my own peace of mind and also for future owners of the home; I think it does give some peace of mind to know things have been done correctly. But when I started I...

Are you implying safety?

Yeah. Like, I do so much research, so much investigation. Any time I start a project, I try to make sure to do it to code. But at the end of the day, I'm—you know, this isn't my profession, so I'm taking a little bit of a risk not doing something correctly, especially in terms of safety for things like earthquakes.

What do you think typifies construction in Los Angeles?

One thing I really appreciate is that you can drive around LA and just find endless variation and inspiration everywhere, which I love. You can find pockets of LA where the designs are so good. Yes, there's also a lot of really horribly done houses, but every time I start a big project, like when I was going to do my kitchen, I would spend my weekends going to open houses and looking at every single corner of a house that's selling for like two million dollars.

That's interesting. So, when you work, do you listen to music, and is there a song or type of music you keep on going back to?

When I first started on the house, I listened to 100.3, which was all classic rock. I listened to it on an old junky, tape player boom box that I think some contractor left at my house. Then it turned into a Christian music station, so I gave up on it. Ever since then, I have listened to audiobooks.

November 8, Brian
(b. 1981)

How did you learn your trade?

I was born in Scotland where two of my uncles were contractors. I was always interested in carpentry, and I knew in the long run I would own my own construction company. My first job was as an apprentice welder in a warehouse. It was cold, and I was working with steel. I found it very depressing; it just wasn't for me.

Around then, my dad's friend—a very good carpenter—lost his driver's license, and I was asked to drive him to work in England every Monday through Friday. It was a Scottish company working for British Gas. I think at the time he only had eight jobs a week.

I watched everything he was doing. One day I overheard the boss saying, "We're going to have to get another carpenter because we're going to have forty jobs a week. Do you know anyone?" I jumped in and said, "I'm a carpenter." That's how it started. Then my uncle, who lived in Los Angeles came home to Scotland for a surprise party. He said, "I have seven jobs going on, and it's too much. I could really be doing better with you out there."

I always wanted to be in Los Angeles. He's the best contractor. He's obsessed with everything mechanical and everything construction, even more than I am. He was only ever going to do one thing, even though he's capable of doing anything.

What year was that?

In 2008, right before the crash, before the recession. I had first come out to Los Angeles to help him for a few months in 2006, and then I moved out permanently in 2008. We did the Project7Ten House, on Abbot Kinney in Venice. It was the first LEED Platinum house in the area, so that was a very, very popular project. A lot of celebrities were involved in the

PR because it was the first luxury green home.

Then my uncle and I worked on a three-story house with a basement next to the beach. The basement was below the water table, which was tricky. I learned everything I could possibly learn about construction at that time. I also had to learn how it is in America—the codes and the way things are done are completely different than in Scotland and England.

What was the transition for you to become a licensed general contractor?

When the market started to pick up again, I found a Craigslist—posted by a commercial building company looking for someone to be a trainee superintendent—and it was only 10 minutes from my house. During the interview, they put some plans down in front of me that I felt very comfortable reading.

Right then and there they told me they wanted me to start. Immediately I was on a Fresh Brothers job in West Hollywood, which is a very popular pizza chain out here. That was my first building.

What was it called?

Fresh Brothers, F-R-E-S-H. They do a gluten-free pizza. They got very popular because the Kardashians would go there on the show. I think it was going to be a five-month to six-month build: It was a 2,000 square foot project.

What was it like working on that project?

Over here people say, “if someone does commercial, that’s it,” they don’t do residential, and vice-versa; it’s very rare to do both. I had never done commercial before, but that kind of project made sense to me. In theory, it’s more difficult because there are more codes, all the ADA compliances, the health department, and so many ins and outs. But for some reason, it was like I already knew 50 percent of it, and then I was just picking up everything else really easy. I built that Fresh Brothers in three months, and it was the fastest one the company had ever done. They were all about speed. I was made a general superintendent, which meant that within just a few weeks of starting they had put me in charge of all the superintendents.

Every job I was in charge of, I would look at the plans for an hour and remember everything that needed to be done. I basically worked my way up with that company, and I was making a good salary.

Then the guy in charge sent me to build-out the first Grimaldi’s Pizzeria in California. They were having trouble getting it moving, and I really turned it around. Everything went well. I got offered a job through someone else who was doing a project next door who noticed when that Grimaldi’s job started going. I ended up getting in with a company called Global Construction where I would earn my first six-figure salary just for being an on-site guy. I started working with Engine Construction, owned and managed by an architect and a developer. I did all the work, but they pulled the contracts as the owner/builder. Eventually I got my contractor’s license. I still do work for them, but also things on my own. I have worked on a lot of amazing projects.

How do you stay competitive?

I have no employees, which means I’m exempt from worker’s comp, so I just subcontract everything out. I work with the same subs again and again, and they are all friendly now and communicate really well. It’s a really good team. Everything I do comes through referrals.

My really long-term goal is to be in the position where I can start to buy property. My goal is to not have to answer to anybody. I’m still chasing the idea of answering to no one. It would mean me buying the property, hiring the architect, deciding what gets done, how it gets built, and doing the work.

Hats off to you for holding on and getting a hold in the market here.
What is it like to build in LA?

... That's actually really easy for me to answer, although I always had that passion for building, back home it was just a job: you don't make a whole lot of money, the weather's terrible and every building is brick with metal stud framing inside. It's just depressing. I love Scotland for what it is, but it wasn't for me. Here, when I think of building, I think: framing with a compressed air nail gun, the noise that it makes with the sun shining, and no top on. On top of that, everyone I meet is fascinated by development and construction. Everybody that walks by with their dogs wants to know what you're building. Everybody wants to know the price per square foot.

When you say "price per square foot," you're talking about the cost of construction?

Yeah, exactly. They always want to know because it seems like everybody wants a piece of real estate at some point. There is a feeling like construction is part of everyone's life to some extent. I remember being mesmerized by Home Depot. It sounds crazy, but I was. I loved the way that it smelled, and there were so many people.

November 8, Marcos
(b. 1963)

How did you learn your trade?

I grew up in Tijuana, where I learned from my uncle, who was a traveling builder and had many skills. At the age of 22, I came to Los Angeles and was doing finish carpentry, and then started working for the company I work for now. I was doing carpentry for eight years, and in 1993, I decided to go into drywall framing. Two years later I became the foreman. I did the Hollywood Bowl. Now I work for galleries on the weekends.

Do you enjoy that kind of work?

Yeah. I get to use a lot of special techniques to make walls with interesting shapes, angles, radiuses, and things like that. On some projects, I'll spend three or four weekends working. If it's a lot of work, I'll leave some of my guys working into the week, but normally just Saturday and Sunday, or Friday or Monday, and that's it.

What does "best practice" mean to you?

When you come to the job, and you grab the plans, you can see everything: walls, windows, ceilings, the reception area. You can see it in your mind. It's when you arrive, and you know how to do almost anything, almost everything. You need to have the experience to give a solution to the architect or the superintendent, or anybody in charge of the project.

The problem is when something doesn't match—elevations, alignments, or something like that. You need to find the problem before you finish. That could be a problem, okay. Let's go back to the architect, okay.

So, you anticipate problems, and then you do something about it.

Yeah, exactly. It helps that I'm good at math. My uncle taught me trigonometry, algebra, and calculus. In the end, I went to college and studied civil engineering.

In Tijuana?

In Tijuana, yeah.

So, you built on that?

Yeah, yeah.

Tell me, what is it like being a builder in Los Angeles?

Here, there's a lot of competition. There's a lot of good builders. When they were building the Disney Concert Hall, another company was working on it. But one day, a friend called

... me and said, "Marcos, I need somebody to help me with layout." "Okay," I said, "I will come for one day only." It was not my company, but he was my friend. "Okay, Marcos, I have this radius, and I have this, and I have that." And I said, "Look, open your mind. You need to look at everything, all the spaces," and we figured it out. I have the ability to look at everything.

Do you think construction is more specialized in America than in Tijuana?

Yes, everyone here is a specialist, like a doctor. General doctors do everything, yeah? Some doctors only look at eyes. But others look at eyes, fingers, stomachs...

That's why I'd say I'm a general carpenter. I can do anything.

November 8, Joe
(b. 1957)

How did you learn your trade?

Thru a lot of mistakes. I learn backwards. I don't learn from the front forward. I first started doing remodeling jobs, so I was tearing things apart before building them.

Were you tearing apart your own property?

The only property I've ever owned is this little tiny shop on a little piece of property. I have chickens—you can probably hear them in the background—and a bunch of fruit trees. I'm next to Zuma Beach, and it's a pretty nice little place.

Do you ever work on homes?

I've worked mostly on high-end homes, a lot of musicians, movie stars, billionaires... My brother is also a contractor, and I work with him a lot. I can just segue into his thing, and it's no big deal. I have a general contractor's license, and he also has a license.

A friend showed me photos of a John Lautner house that you had worked on.

I just finished that Lautner house last February. It was an 800 square foot house. That one was a real pickle. The owners bought it, and tried to return it to its original state, which was a big job. They didn't even really change any of it. But the people that had done work on it a while back in previous renovation, like in a lot of these houses that we do, people have their own vision. Everybody thinks they're the architect. Even though the architect on this job wrote a book about Lautner...

What does "best practice" mean to you?

I think "always trying to achieve perfection." To me, everything is about quality, not the amount of work you do; it's the quality. I don't like cutting corners.

What do you think about houses here in Los Angeles?

We're basically just stick framers out here. But they don't have a school; they don't have any technical institutes in America. The guilds are gone, so people just learn on the job like I did. Then you choose the direction you want to go.

When did the guilds end?

What I mean is there are unions—carpenters unions and union schools. They're still here, but they're just not as prevalent because people just want to get stuff done. A lot of problems with the houses in LA, especially in desirable areas, is that there's so much money and construction in California—especially down in LA—and people don't want to wait for that carpenter or this contractor or that architect. Then they run into problems because those jobs go to people that just say, "I can do that." But they really don't have the experience. I can't tell you how many jobs my brother takes on where they have to go

... in because someone forgot to put window pans and door pans in, the water's leaking into the finished house after four years.

I tell people I'm not really a great carpenter, but I know what looks good: I know what needs to be done to get it there, but I'm not really that good. I'm good enough to tell you what it's going to take to make it happen. That's the absolute truth.

Do you think you can get away with a bit more because there's not much rain?

Absolutely. If we had more rain, if we lived in England, for example, construction would be much different. There would be more details about waterproofing and roofing. We just get by and go with what looks good from afar.

I was working on a house on Malibu Road for a doctor with a big architect. They came, and they said, "Joe, we want you to put mahogany capping on this metal railing outside." It was a concrete and steel house, real industrial looking. They had this thin piece of metal going from post-to-post, then they were going to put the wood on top and then screw it to the thin piece of metal. I told them the wood would last for about two weeks, but then after that it would look like it had been in the ocean. The architect looked at me and said, "I'm the architect; you're the carpenter."

Two weeks later, my contractor friend came and said, "Joe, you're right, let's do it the way you said." We deal a lot with that because architects have huge egos. I don't know if you know that or not. Huge.

Yeah?

But being right is a shallow victory.

I agree.

Sometimes it's better to shut your mouth. But a lot of the time, like I said, when people are spending money, and you know it's not right, you have to... it's not a winning thing. You want the project to be good for the owner, the people that are spending the money because it's a lot of money. We're talking lots and lots of money. I don't make that kind of money.

It's a classic paradigm, the wrestle that goes on between contractor and architect, and I think that is actually important. If someone was going to build a house here in Los Angeles, do you have any advice?

Think it through. I think it's really important for anybody doing any building to really spend the time researching what they want and get it down. Once you start changing, it starts costing a lot of money. A lot of people have so much money; they just change every week. That's fine for a while, but that stuff gets boring.

People buy a house, and then they change it from a Spanish revival to a modern house. Money means nothing to them, which is kind of so gauche. Good materials, which is what I usually get, are getting harder and harder to find. I think it's important for people to spend time looking at what they want, setting their goals, then doing it and not changing it.

Trace Contaminants

Wendy Gilmartin

A million gaskets, screws, valves, pads, slots, pins, threads, perforations, and tubes are pressed, grouped, smashed, weighed, dropped, burned, turned, tossed, and thoroughly assessed for uniformity, radial spread, limit of compaction, limit of compression, and thresholds of minimal and maximum difference. Testing parameters are set too. A heat input of 50 kW/m2 burns at the distance of 12 inches from a square meter of horizontally oriented material not exceeding 1-inch thickness for a period of ten minutes. Carpet will tend to smolder at nine minutes. Cardboard at three minutes. Out of these granular variable sets, which accumulate and grow to become metadata, reference standards are penned. Acceptable ranges are established as criteria for approval of actual nuts and honest-to-goodness bolts.

See: ASTM E1995, Standard Test Method for Measurement of Smoke Obscuration Using a Conical Radiant Source in a Single Closed Chamber, With the Test Specimen Oriented Horizontally.

A thousand turbines, elevators, houses, and office buildings take shape from accumulated steel fasteners and rubber washers, plywood sheets, nails, whole truck beds of metal decking, blades, coils, conduit, pre-primed decorative wood trims, switches, and vents. All are checked again and again for tightness, sound transmission, air leakage, heat gain, pressure control, and systems performance.

To fall within the acceptable range of referenced standards.

In the "age of the world spreadsheet," the maintenance of property values, assets, building components, and their continuous marketability happens via the controls of budget and time. Safeguards are developed to eliminate failures and vulnerabilities. Doing so involves establishing goals and objectives. Gathering relevant information. Identifying strategies. Determining quantitative requirements. Meeting agendas, conference calls, meeting minutes, base lines, bench marks, quality checks, field reports, summaries, action items, revisions, resolutions, compromises, adjustments, version 2.0, reissues, waiting lines, weight limits, focus groups, evaluations, sales, passcodes, key codes, bar codes, scan codes, time codes, trash day, casual Fridays, birthday cakes in the break room. Hinging on safeguards to eliminate failures and

Generally, this refers to a world view driven by the affordances of a data-centric matrix-based workspace, more specifically however "The Age of the World Spreadsheet" was a seven-day performance series by Steve Kado at Machine Project in Los Angeles "examining the roots and conclusions of rationality's capacity and the vile glory of our human limits." [https://machineproject.com/2010/events/age-of-the-world-spreadsheet/]

... vulnerabilities, the litany of placements, findings, and rollouts are subject to repeated change.

Project workflows manifest via the order of filled—and yet-unfilled—cells in Microsoft's Excel tablature. Colored boxes within a matrix correspond to previously determined criteria sets. "Within maximum amounts of contaminant radiation allowed in drinking water per the EPA-approved analytical methods for measuring radionuclides in drinking water report of 1998?" Marked "yes." "Got the appropriate gage thickness of a corner radius sheet metal drain pipe per ASTM section A924/A924M?" Marked "yes." This is a dance designed to avoid as many freestyle moves as possible. To expertly evade a distillation of the infinite complexity of possibilities within a constantly churning matrix of deterioration and resurrection.

Best practices create the conditions through which a method of organized, controlled, and to-be-met criteria checks in and lands its final leg of the long journey from processing plant to pre-approved placement. All prior and respective approvals can be reviewed, and now they tick towards the critical path of execution in physical time and space. Such is the thin binary essence that maintains contractual agreements between owner and operator, buyer and seller, laborer and industry professional, governance and citizenry. The paper trail. The standard. The standard of care.❤

❤ See: Architects Practice Act Business and Professions Code Chapter 3, Division 3 of the California Code of Regulations Title 16, Division 2.

The project manager is master of the budget and of the timeline, the master spreadsheet cell filler whose lingo is industry standard, middle tone; polite yet chilly emails always follow up, and are archived. His standard of care is made explicit with nowhere to hide. His approach: a craven middle ground destination of tonal mean value, with little curve or intonation. Risk is managed.

- - - - - -

When the day's work is done, folks head to a watering hole smack in the middle of a hot, asphalt parking lot at 11665 Victory Boulevard, North Hollywood. Captain's Cabin has no windows and even less decoration. The paint is peeling. Two orange, classical-ish columns support a triangular overhang above the entrance. Thick vertical strips of yellowed plastic hang where the door would normally be. The Cabin has been there for over 35 years. People have fun there and spend money. Everyday stresses and worries are dropped at the door and exchanged for rounds of cold beer and dance. Music blares until 2 a.m. Dim red and green lights make everyone look a little more interesting. Neighbors close their windows. The place gets hosed out in the morning.

... Technically this gritty tip of North Hollywood is described in city documents as "a district in the San Fernando Valley region of the City of Los Angeles." The area looks vaguely rural, but crowded too, with scattered yet ordered rows of pot shops, parking lots, used car lots with fluttering, metallic flags. In the North Valley, there are many neighborhoods like this one. This is the place Arthur Schlesinger imagined in 1940:

> "When the city encroaches sufficiently on the country and the country on the city, there will come an opportunity for the development of a type of civilization such as the world has never known. The old hard-and-fast distinction between urban and rural will tend to disappear."✸

The neighborhood around Vineland and Victory is a place where people aren't always free to make their own choices about appearance or disappearance. And yet, it's a territory of pronounced individualism and stealthy subversion amidst exquisite, confounding mistakes.

Along the street there's a feeble but considerate wooden garden trellis attempting to screen rooftop air conditioning equipment from tenants below. Six different shades of light blue paint make a pattern on a parking lot wall where each coat was dedicated to covering up a new set of territorial tagging. A plastic owl perched on a metal awning is there to keep pigeons away. Sinewy, stuck-on grab bars, metal ramp, and handrail additions to a house indicate the presence of someone ailing or infirm. A 20-foot-tall, bright orange inflatable tube with a smiling face and tassels for hair, it's air-blower powered engine sending it high in the blowing hot valley air, bends and gyrates desperately for attention to the building behind. The AM radio in a passing car pops and hisses,

> "Ever notice when your neighbors get new windows, there's a large blemish of broken stucco, uneven plaster, and mismatched paint?... We call that 'ring around the window'... We never leave a ring around the window... Everyone else on the radio is a distributor. They grab a window from a warehouse, break open your walls, shove it in, and patch things up... Our proprietary installation system is so precise, your house could be covered with potato chips and we wouldn't crack one chip!"

The bit is from an advertisement for California Deluxe Windows. The invoked image of a house covered in potato chips has garnered the company's owner, Latvian immigrant Aaron Adrim, a degree

✸ See: Arthur M. Schlesinger, "The City in American History," Mississippi Valley Historical Review, Vol. 27, No. 1 (Jun., 1940), 43–66.

… of local celebrity. He has been dubbed "the Potato Chip Guy," and he now "stars" in his own advertisements set out to target a more upscale consumer that focuses more on quality and less on price. The advertisement's easy explanation of the product describes the value of local production, quality assurance, and a manufacturing process that eliminates multiple providers by also acting as the installer. These elements are what elevate Adrim's vinyl windows above his competitors' brand—and above those inept builders who would otherwise break the precious stucco on your potato chip house.

\- - - - - -

Schlesinger's encroaching end hereby spans the horizon of LA, its economy, its history, and its art. The best process (practice?) through which to document the spanning end—with its windows, drainpipes, concert halls, and freeways, its workers, celebrities, and murders—has confounded and intrigued artists and photographers from David Alfaro Siqueiros, Leonard Nadel, and Kent MacKenzie, to James Benning, Gary Leonard, Catherine Opie, and Alan Sekula. Sekula outlined the elusive hunt for honest materiality in his 1999 lecture "Los Angeles: Graveyard of Documentary," emphasizing,

> "The reoccurring tropes of economic life [in Los Angeles] are hyperbolic, they oscillate between utopia and dystopian extremes. The overriding image is that of the gamble, of speculative risk. Consequently, the representation of 'what is' is always liable to be judged as miserably inferior to 'what could be' or 'what is just around the corner.'" ⚐

Ed Ruscha's *A Few Palm Trees* (1971) offers an intentionally incomplete survey of isolated, non-native trees in Los Angeles. In their presentation, sheathed within a 64-page pamphlet, their unobscured mundanity pushes a prose of the unremarkable. Robert Smithson also took to isolated viewing in an "anti-expedition" to the Yucatan in 1969. The immersive trip yielded a critique of traditional travel narratives and site analysis, calling into question the means of viewing such destinations. Smithson called this methodology of seeing "dedifferentiation," the absorption of landscapes via simplified, receptive steps: "The eyes became two wastebaskets filled with diverse colors, variegations, ashy hues, blotches, and sunburned chromatics." ✺ With the help of half-buried mirrors that he scattered at the base of Mayan ruins, the surrounding landscape was not viewed or pictured but delineated through an accretive convergence.

⚐ Alan Sekula's lecture was first presented at the University of Southern California, as the second of three Getty Lectures, March 1997. Revised for the Opler Lecture delivered at Harvard University on April 15, 1999.

✺ See: Robert Smithson, "Incidents of Mirror-Travel in the Yucatan," in Robert Smithson and Nancy Holt Papers, Archives of American Art, Smithsonian Institution, Washington, D.C., and New York., "1969a," 119-33. (1969). From the research of Jennifer L. Roberts, The Art Bulletin, Vol. 82, No. 3 (Sep., 2000), 544-567.

... The images and captions in Erin Besler and Ian Besler's Best Practices are somewhat like Smithson's work in the Yucatan: a sort of low-level scan. Strip retail centers, grates, gates, and doorways reveal provisional elements of constructed space as anachronisms instead of what they were intended to be—substitutions or solutions. The text offers a phrenic pivot. The consequential residues of mass-produced, market-driven products, as they've been applied by cheap construction means and methods in Los Angeles, are shown again differently on the next page. Like Ruscha's palm trees, the road cones, tinted glass, and HVAC units are prose-like but aren't an index. Nor are they a celebration of bricolage or the ad-hoc.

We take the dog to the vet in an ugly building with funny drain pipes. Our local bank branch looks like a Taco Bell. The grocery store is also a giant stucco box. We live in "the 99%" of structures born of real estate development status quo norms and project managers' best practices. They are safe, inoffensive (read: beige), and easily repeatable. Most of these buildings aren't created by teams of architects, nor are they protected by boards of preservationists or boosted by critics from large newspapers. Placed in a book or in a gallery—or even on an Instagram page—extractions from the 99% transform: they become isolated, detached from context, dissectible, differently meaningful, and disaffected. Are we looking with indifference, or are we looking in deference? With pathos or potentiality? In isolating mistakes and accommodations (with their implicated contaminations), we might simultaneously consider the contractor's timeline, the owner's value-engineering, the contingency, the neighbors, the dignity of building something, the privilege of looking awry.

In dedifferentiating the altered landscape of LA, shuffled glimpses coalesce a distinguishable peripheral methodology—one no doubt gone astray from standard procedures. In so doing, a stake is claimed, advocating an oppositional practice that hangs somewhere between demolition and renewal. Mistakes and misplacements, covered-up accidents, eyeballing it, and jerry-rigged prostheses are now materialized as a tidily taped up call box or a woman's manicured likeness upon a window decal (terribly sliced across her cornea by storefront mullions). A haphazard array of DirecTV dishes resembles a clump of mushrooms, germinating from an apartment building's stucco frontage along Eagle Rock Boulevard. It is something insouciant and unplanned. It is something.

\- - - - - -

Wendy Gilmartin

Acknowledgments

This work is built upon the suggestions and insights generously shared by colleagues, students, and friends from the worlds of architecture on the one hand and interaction design on the other. We both pursued our graduate degrees in Southern California, Erin in Architecture and Ian in Media Design, and we brought these divergent interests together in Downtown Los Angeles to establish our practice, Besler & Sons, which is informed as much by the city and its buildings as by the individuals that have given them shape. We are incredibly grateful to the many people and institutions that have supported this project over its five years of development. And while the extent to which Los Angeles informed our work cannot be understated: a project of this nature is not produced in one place, alone, or at a single moment in time, but through collaborations and conversations in cities and small towns around the world, with both casual observers and experts alike. We have been fortunate to share time and attention with so many people and have been humbled by the generosity and support of the many considerate thinkers and prolific creators to whom we will forever be indebted.

In July 2015, an email with the subject line "Book?" arrived in our inbox. Over coffee a few days later, Jonathan Jae-an Crisman proposed that a series of photographs, wrenched from the ether of social media and given extended investigation with captions, could be the basis for a published work. Although the lead time and scope expanded a bit, we are thankful to him for the initial nudge, the friendly encouragement, and his inexhaustible reserves of interest in the book, the spirit of which he wonderfully captured in his contribution.

We are incredibly grateful to Sylvia Lavin for introducing this book with words and ideas that have made it more robust and intelligible. Her insight, generous feedback, and ongoing conversations have given clarity, shape, and purpose to the images and texts we've put forward.

Our continued collaborations with Fiona Connor have strengthened our recognition of the more nuanced material, social, and institutional systems that construct cities and spaces. We are appreciative of the conversations with builders she has shared here and the knowledge they transmit.

We'd like to thank Wendy Gilmartin for the incisive insights in her written contribution, which waited patiently in a folder on our hard drives while we continued to write and rewrite this book.

This publication, which brought a new space of circulation and new meaning to this collection of images and text, would not have been possible without generous support from The Graham Foundation for Advanced Studies in the Fine Arts, support that arrived at a crucial time in the project.

Many thanks to Jake Anderson and the dedicated team at AR+D/ORO whose interest and support for the project, despite the slow build and extended schedule, never faltered.

Courtney Coffman's sharp editorial eye and intellectual agility made comprehensible a collection of texts on disparate subjects, tangential readings, less recognized forms of production, and not-so-conventional formatting. We appreciate the attention and care she devoted to the project.

Much of the writing and image selection would not have been possible without Christina Moushoul, whose creative capacity as a research assistant and associate editor was

... essential. In particular, conversations with Christina in the spring and summer of 2020 kept us hopeful and motivated when the global and national circumstances seemed to insist otherwise.

Sarah Hearne has been a consistent sounding board on more aspects of this project than we can count, providing the much-needed, astute, and honest critique that is often hard to garner.

We're appreciative of the colleagues, students, faculty, and friends who we first met in Los Angeles at the Southern California Institute of Architecture, and UCLA's Department of Architecture and Urban Design, whose reactions and responses along the way seemed encouraging—or at least, not completely averse to the ideas and images we've circulated—including Greg Lynn, Neil Denari, Katy Barkan, Margo Handwerker, Michael Osman, Jason Payne, Julia Körner, Jimenez Lai, Kristy Balliet, Maya Alam, David Eskenazi, Andrew Atwood, Anna Neimark, Joanna Grant, Jia Gu, Matt Au, and Russell Thomsen.

Observations and sharper ways of thinking were provided by faculty, advisors, students, and fellows in the Media Design Practices program at ArtCenter College of Design in Pasadena, the Roski School of Art and Design at the University of Southern California, and the Design Technology Department at Santa Monica College, including Ben Hooker, Jenny Rodenhouse, Tim Durfee, Benjamin Bratton, Anne Burdick, Kevin Wingate (who first suggested the name for our office, Besler & Sons, if only as an affectionate joke, nevertheless it stuck and has served us well), Haven Lin-Kirk, Jeff Cain, Elise Co, Mimi Zeiger, Norman Klein, Luke Johnson, Garnet Hertz, David Leonard, Casey Anderson, Andrew Nagata, Hugo Pilates, Aaron Fooshée, and many others.

Los Angeles is the beguiling and quirky metropolis it is today because, among so many other events, a group known in the film industry as the "independents" left New Jersey for Southern California in order to get some distance from Thomas Edison and his Motion Picture Patent Company's monopoly on the industry. It's fitting, if not ironic, that we wrote most of this book in New Jersey following our relocation from Los Angeles. Our move in the other direction was under a different pretense and by no means independent, but the change of coasts has been impactful nonetheless. We are grateful for the institutional, intellectual, and creative support provided by the Princeton University School of Architecture. This book is propelled by impromptu conversations, in-depth discussions, probing prompts, and sidebar chats with colleagues including Dean Mónica Ponce de León, Forrest Meggers, Mario Gandelsonas, Jesse Reiser, Stan Allen, Liz Diller, Paul Lewis, Christine Boyer, Michael Meredith, Guy Nordenson, Beatriz Colomina, Marshall Brown, Cameron Wu, Spyros Papapetros, Mitch McEwen, Lucia Allais, Ivi Diamantopoulou, and Stefana Parascho.

The built environment is constantly being written and rewritten. The idea that the specifics of a particular place are not defined by one physical location, but rather by the constellation and accumulation of forces surrounding it, both visible and invisible, was reinforced during our time spent at the American Academy in Rome when in residence during Erin's Rome Prize Fellowship in Architecture. We would like to express our gratitude to the Academy for the time, space, and support that enabled us to venture out with our iPhones to conduct research. Our shared interests were shaped not only by Rome, its inhabitants, and its environs, but by the conversations across fields and interests from sculpture, conservation, history, photography, archaeology, and graphic design, to architecture, gender studies, performance art, economics, religion, and popular culture, with Lori Wong, Karyn Olivier, Kirstin Valdez Quade, Franco Baldasso, Joannie Bottkol, Anna Majeski, Marcel Sanchez Prieto, Amy Franceschini, Allison Emmerson, Mark Letteney, David Ogawa, Peter Benson Miller, John Ochsendorf, Mark Robbins, Lynne Lancaster, Lindsay Harris, Giuliana Bruno, Andrew Freiberg, Alice Friedman, Marlon Blackwell, Marion Weiss, Michael Manfredi, and Pippo Ciorra.

Lastly, we'd like to thank our parents Sherri and Michael, Barbara and Harry. Besler & Sons is at its most fundamental level a family practice, and we are so grateful for the many ways that our family has shown up to support our work and contribute to it.

Best Practices